A TRANSFORMATIVE JOURNEY THROUGH TRAUMA TO TRIUMPH

RESTORING THE YEARS

Thanks for
being part of
the journey
:)

egrace

ESTHER GRACE

FIRST EDITION

ISBN: 978-1-7384132-6-3 (Paperback)

Restoring the Years is published by TC Publishing

Content Warning - This memoir discusses themes of sexual abuse which some readers may find distressing or triggering.

Disclaimer - This memoir is based on true events. Names and identifying details have been changed to protect the privacy of individuals involved, unless otherwise noted.

Illustrations by Carys Wynne-Jones

For information, please direct emails to:

info@tc-publishing.com

TC PUBLISHING

Contents

Acknowledgements

Firstly, I'd like to say a massive thank you to Carys. Thank you for your diligence and determination in creating the beautiful illustrations for this book. It's a blessing to have your artwork displayed in these pages.

I'd like to thank Jess, the amazing lady who helped proofread and edit this book. Thank you for the hours of hard work and dedication you put into it. I appreciate you. Your consistent encouragement and sensitivity really did make it a pleasure to work with you.

I want to acknowledge Peter, Emily, Fiona, Ebony and Hayley, who also helped with proofreading. Thanks, guys! The proofreading process definitely felt like a team effort, and I'm thankful so many of you were willing to support me with it.

Thank you to everyone who has played a part in the making and releasing of this book. Thank you to those who gave financially. Thank you to those who prayed. And thank you to those who have encouraged and supported me on this book-writing adventure.

I'm blessed with many great friends, some of whom you're going to read about in the chapters that follow. I have so many amazing friends that it wasn't possible to mention all of them in this book. However, I would like to acknowledge that I am extremely thankful to each and every one of you! You have all been a blessing to my life, and I'm thankful to God that you're a part of my story.

Last but definitely not least, I have to say a massive thank you to Jesus. This book wouldn't have been possible without You.

INTRODUCTION

Hey, I'm so thankful that you've taken the opportunity to pick up and read this book.

I'm sharing these stories from my life with you in the hope that they encourage you to believe that no matter how dark your past and present may be, there is always hope. I understand how cliché that statement can sound when you're in a dark place mentally, but one of the things I've learnt through writing this book is the importance of reflecting on how far you've come. My life isn't perfect, and neither am I, but as you read this book, I hope you will start to dream and believe that change truly is possible, and that unconditional acceptance and love really do have the power to bring transformation.

I genuinely believe that as you read through these pages, you will receive a fresh revelation of the power and presence of God. For some, I'm aware that even reading that sentence could trigger challenging emotions and thoughts; but I want to encourage you to see that whether you know God or not, there will be something in this book that speaks to you.

Disclaimer The stories I have recounted in this book are written from my perspective, and I have kept them as true to reality as possible. However, I have changed most of the names of people and places. I also want to make you aware that some of the experiences shared in this book are graphic and detailed, and may not be appropriate for children; parental guidance is advised. Some adults may also find the content challenging and/or triggering.

I have included a small list of websites and organisations at the back of this book for anyone who may be struggling.

I have also written a small prayer that you could read aloud (if you feel comfortable to) before beginning:

Father God,

I pray that as I read this book, You would open my heart to hear what You may be saying to me. Please bring healing from my past so that I can live in the fullness of what You have for me. Encourage me, strengthen me, and help me to see and know that there is hope and a future for me.

In Jesus' name, I pray,

Amen.

CHAPTER 1: SEPARATION

My story begins in July 1993. I was born weighing 6lb 3oz at a hospital in Greater Manchester, UK. I loved hearing my mum's account of how I was brought into the world. Upside down, the wrong way around. They pushed me back in and turned me around as my mum screamed a few profanities at me and others in the room.

She often told me how thrilled she was when she found out I was a girl. She'd always wanted a daughter. She'd say that the pain she went through in childbirth was nothing compared to the way she felt when she held me in her arms for the very first time.

I'd love to say that the childhood years following my birth were full of joy and laughter and that I grew up happily with my parents and three brothers, but that's not how the story went.

My mum and dad didn't exactly have the healthiest of relationships. They were besotted with one another to begin with, but as time went on, they started arguing and fighting. They both drank and dabbled with drugs, but my mum's main difficulty came in the form of the mental health challenges she faced due to abuse and unresolved trauma from her past. It feels important for me to mention that neither of my parents were bad people. However, their struggles did significantly impact their ability to raise and look after me and my siblings.

Most of us have memories from childhood — some earlier than others. I have an exceptionally good recollection of events, starting from a really young age. I remember being bathed in the sink, my mum brushing my hair, and going out in the pram to the local shops. I have a vivid memory of being in the pram under a rain cover, with the raindrops bouncing off it and my mind not quite understanding how I wasn't getting wet. I have so many beautiful memories from my early years, but for a long time, I could only remember the negative ones.

My mum told me that I'd gone into care at the age of one and how I struggled to settle in the new foster placement. I stood, staring at the door whilst crying uncontrollably, refusing to be consoled by anyone other than my mum. The foster parents called my mum for advice, but nothing they did seemed to comfort me. I stopped crying instantly when my mum showed up and took me home with her for a few days. But she soon became mentally unwell again, and I ended up back in the care system.

As a toddler, I remember being laid on the back seat of a social worker's car, screaming and violently kicking the window with my feet. I didn't understand why I was being taken away from my mum again. Before I left, she brought out a man (my new stepdad) to introduce me to him. I remember being so upset and questioning why she was choosing him over me. That was my childlike way of interpreting it. But I know now there was far more to the situation than I could comprehend.

Although I don't fully remember the process of going into care and everything that happened, I do remember the overwhelming desire I had to see and be with my mum again.

I realise now the importance of secure attachment in the early years of anyone's life and how the toing and froing and the back and forth from my mum to different foster carers made it difficult for me to form healthy relationships with others as a child. I was sometimes very clingy with adults and caregivers for fear of them leaving me. This meant I was often focused on grown-ups and getting my needs met instead of trying to interact and make friends with children my age. I didn't receive adequate support in the area of attachment as a child, so understandably, it was an issue that continued into my early adult life. I'll explain more about my healing journey with attachment later in the book.

I was around 5 years old when Social Services and the court decided to put me and my siblings on a full care order. My younger brother and I were kept together and placed with a family in Liverpool. However, my two older brothers were placed in separate foster families. We were all supposed to live with these new families until we were 18. But for three of us, it didn't quite work out that way.

I was still allowed to speak to my mum and brothers on the phone regularly, but contact with my dad was nearly non-existent. Face-to-face visits with my mum and siblings could take place up to six times a year. But it never felt like enough. I just couldn't understand why it wasn't possible for us all to live together like a 'normal' family. One of the consolations I had was that I still had my little brother Liam with me. There are only ten and a half months between us in age, so we always felt quite close growing up. I honestly had a lot of good times in the foster home in Liverpool. Liam and I often played on the pylon outside, made up games on the local estate with the other kids, and traipsed around the local pub grounds to see if we could find any money. I feel like I was a relatively smiley and upbeat child, considering the awfulness that my brother and I were experiencing.

At such a young age, I didn't recognise that the way we were being treated was wrong. I just thought it was 'normal'. I thought that most kids got beaten if they said or did things wrong or if things like making your bed and folding your clothes weren't done to a good enough standard. I began to realise how wrong this was when a disabled boy was placed in the foster family, and because he couldn't do things 'well enough', he would regularly be beaten and taunted. I often helped to do the extra household tasks for him and my brother, and I quickly learned how to do things well from a young age. It felt at the time like my life and happiness depended on it.

Trigger Warning – Sexual Abuse

There's no way to sugarcoat what happened next...

Basil, the man who was supposed to be a new dad to me, took advantage of my innocence and abused it. He coerced me into doing sexual acts for money, sweets and affection.

Not only did he do that, but he managed to make me believe that it was all my idea and that it wasn't abuse because I had willingly said yes.

Looking back now from a place of having worked through that trauma, I realise how warped that thinking was. I had genuinely believed that it wasn't abuse because I'd said yes. It took years of therapy and support from friends for me to fully believe that what had happened to me was abuse. As a child, I didn't have the capacity to be making decisions around sexual activity. He had manipulated, groomed and abused me.

The abuse continued for a few years until one evening, Liam stumbled downstairs and saw what was happening to me. The following morning, we went to school as usual. But at the end of that day, a social worker was at the gates to collect us. Liam had bravely told his teacher about what he had seen, and thankfully, we were moved from that placement that very same day (the incident triggered a formal investigation — no charges were brought against Basil).

I was around 8 when we were moved back to Manchester and placed in emergency accommodation. I'd stayed in contact with my mum and brothers, but my eldest brother Ian was slowly starting to speak to and see us less. I assumed it was because his new foster family was working out well, but I wasn't fully sure of the reasons why the contact with him decreased and then suddenly stopped. For years, I was jealous and bitter about his 'new' family. But now, I can honestly say I'm happy that he found a family unit where he was kept safe and where he felt he belonged.

Up to this point, Liam and I had experienced an array of foster homes. Social Services informed us that they were struggling to find us a long-term foster placement, mostly due to our age, but also because they wanted to place us in a home together. Many foster carers and adoptive parents are looking for a baby or a young child, not 8-year-old siblings who'd been in the care system for years. So, with seemingly no other options, they placed us in a children's home in Greater Manchester.

It wasn't as bad as I thought it was going to be. Well, the first children's home, that is. I still have fond memories of the fun times I had there. We'd go on day trips, which involved things like walking up mountains, collecting seashells at the beach, and sledging when it snowed. One specific memory I have is from a local garden party. I got to dress up in a beautiful pink princess dress, and I helped to run a 'Play Your Cards Right' stall. I enjoyed helping with the stall, but was far more interested in trying to win a goldfish and dancing around in my pretty pink dress.

Amidst all the fun times, there were plenty of chaotic moments, too! There was a TV programme called 'Tracy Beaker' at the time about a girl who was in care. It made me laugh, how realistic it was, with the kicking off and the playing tricks on the staff. But living in an actual children's home was much more intense. I can laugh now at many of the things I got up to in care, but when I was living through it, it was exceptionally tough. I didn't understand why I felt things so deeply, why sometimes a slight change or minor inconvenience would trigger a deep and emotional response within me. Now, I realise I hadn't learnt how to emotionally regulate as a child due to the lack of secure attachment and the abuse and trauma I'd faced (and was still facing) in the care system. I was very much in survival mode.

Things felt even more challenging as Liam and I neared puberty. With the mix of emotional difficulties and new hormones, it was understandable why we started arguing and fighting more. However, Social Services felt our behaviour was becoming unmanageable, so decided it would be best for me to be moved somewhere else.

At times, I wondered how differently things might have turned out if Liam and I had been kept together. I often reminded myself that there was no point in hoping and wishing to be reunited with Liam because it wasn't going to happen. Up to that point, the care system had been scary, uncontrollable, challenging and abusive. But I'd always had my little brother close by. What felt like the one 'constant' throughout the whirlwind of my childhood was no longer there, and I was alone in yet another new home.

I was around 10 years old when I got moved to a home not too far from Liam, a children's home where I'd live for the next three years. We still had regular contact, but it wasn't the same as living with him, looking out for him and knowing he was safe. I struggled a lot with the separation, and I know he did, too. Sometimes, I'd lay in bed at night and look at the ceiling, just longing for someone to come and hug me tight and tell me everything was going to be alright. Don't get me wrong, there were times when staff and foster carers did comfort and support me, but there were countless times they didn't, and I was left to manage those big and challenging emotions by myself.

CHAPTER 2: FIGHT! FLIGHT! FREEZE!

At age 11, I felt things were extremely out of control for me. I started running away with some of the older boys from the children's home, and I'd often end up having sex with them. We'd be out all hours of the morning, creating chaos in the local neighbourhood. We'd do dangerous things like run across train tracks, smash windows and jump off rooftops. We ran away so frequently that I couldn't tell you how many times we were reported missing to the police.

Trigger Warning – Suicide Attempt

There were other occasions when I ran away and went to my mum's house. I remember a time I turned up at her house, and she got so drunk that she overdosed in front of me. She kept saying, 'I'm sorry, I don't want to be here anymore', and I remember looking at her through my 11-year-old eyes and seeing how overcome she was with hopelessness and despair. I started panicking, telling myself that I had to do something to help save my mum. I sprang into action, calling 999 for an ambulance before running into the street, screaming. I didn't know how else to let out the pain I was feeling. It felt surreal but scary all at the same time.

Thankfully, they got to my mum quickly, and after a hospital visit, she was well enough to go home again. This dysfunctional relational dynamic between my mum and me went on for the rest of my childhood. I got used to the way things were between us. It wasn't until I became an adult that I realised how unhealthy my relationship was with her and how much false responsibility I had carried in relation to her and my siblings.

I felt such an emptiness within, and no matter how I tried to fill that void throughout my childhood, it just didn't quite satisfy me. I started to cut my arms in a cry for attention, but it soon became an unhealthy coping mechanism. I often drank alcohol as a way of numbing the thoughts in my mind and the intensity of my emotions. But that wasn't a helpful coping mechanism, either.

One thing that did help me was singing. I'd sung to myself and others from a young age and found it brought me comfort, peace and joy. I realise now it was helping me to express my emotions instead of suppressing them. It's also a part of my gifting — to use my voice to not only bring healing to myself but also to others. I've always loved to sing and believe I always will.

The next three years were full of such drastic high and low moments for me. I had lots of fun times when we'd play football in the back garden for hours at a time, as the summer nights meant we could stay out later. I'd make up dance routines and songs with other girls in the home, and we'd put on shows for the staff. I remember taking part in an art project with a local art gallery, too, and our work was put on display for all to see — it was great fun. I remember wanting those fun moments to last forever and often felt a deep disappointment when those experiences came to an end. At that time, I didn't realise that's what was going on for me emotionally. I just knew I felt overwhelmed, and I didn't quite know how to articulate or deal with that. The staff didn't seem to fully recognise what was going on for me, either. Don't get me wrong, there were some staff I got on well with and felt loved and supported by. But I did have an inner struggle of 'if they love me, then why are they leaving me?'. Unlike the consistency of a family unit, which is always there, the staff worked in shifts. So, building healthy attachments in that inconsistent environment was very difficult for me.

Sometimes, I'd cry, scream, or shout when my emotions were too overwhelming. Most of the staff weren't equipped to help me manage the intensity of my emotions, and they regularly used restraint as a way of exerting control over me. I'd get restrained for silly things like not going into another room when asked, putting my elbows on the table, swearing at them, or not wanting to go to bed, etc. They'd tell me to take a bath, and if I didn't want to, they'd physically force me into the tub full of water, holding me down whilst I screamed and fought to get out.

Other incidents involved staff dragging and throwing me into my bedroom and then proceeding to hold the door tightly shut, sometimes for what felt like hours at a time. On one occasion, I threw my TV through the window to escape from the home. I climbed through the broken window, shuffled along the tiny ledge, jumped onto the conservatory, then dangled and dropped to the floor before making a run for it. The staff had me arrested for criminal damage. *But maybe if I'd told the police about how I was being treated, they'd have had a different view on the matter?*

I was arrested on several occasions between the ages of 10 and 13. I found it particularly unhelpful that whenever I was being interviewed by the police, the appropriate adult who had to be present was always a staff member from the children's home, where most of the incidents were taking place. I didn't feel safe enough at that time to tell the whole story because a staff member was in the room with us. So, I often stated 'no comment' throughout the police interviews. I spent hours and days in cells and courtrooms.

I told my mum about the things that were happening, and I'm thankful that she believed me. But whenever she raised it with the staff, they'd tell her that they only used restraint and involved the police as a 'last resort'. I knew that wasn't the case. I hated the injustice of what was going on. I didn't know if things would get worse if I kept telling my mum, so I stopped speaking to her and my social worker about the details of each incident. It somehow felt safer that way.

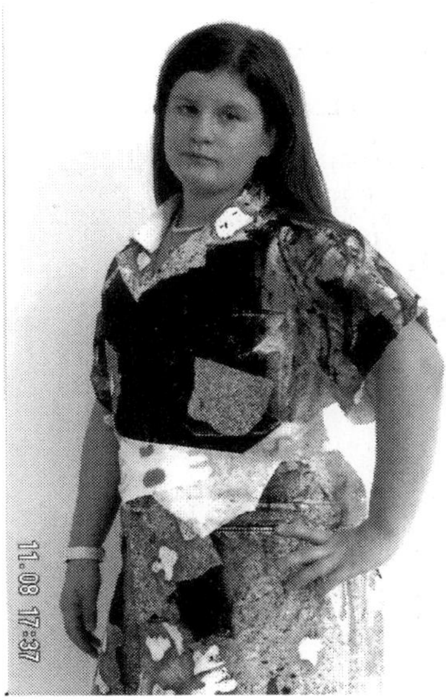

The internal anger I was wrestling with in the children's home began to bubble so ferociously within that it soon started to affect my education, too. Up until that point, I'd always been doing well in school and was always called the clever child. However, I was starting to become verbally abusive in school and was struggling to stay focused in class.

One time, a teacher asked me to leave the classroom because I was talking. I pointed out that lots of other people were talking, so why was she just picking on me? But she continued to ask me to leave the room. I refused, and she proceeded to call a senior teacher to 'remove me' from the classroom. As I walked towards the door, the male teacher tried to grab me and pull me out of the room. My knee-jerk reaction was to fight. I was used to being restrained in the children's home as a form of control, and this situation reminded me of that. So, I kicked and punched him until he let me go. I remember him looking at me and saying, 'You've got so much anger inside of you, haven't you?' and at that time, he was very right.

I didn't go back to the kids' home that day.

I knew I'd be 'sanctioned' for my behaviour, so I got straight on the bus to town and made my way to my mum's. It was just one of those 'I need my mum' moments. She made me some tea, and we chatted about what had happened at school that day. Not long after being there, I knew the time would come when my mum would have to call the police to let them know I'd turned up at her house. They'd come and get me and take me back to the kids' home. I knew the drill, although it didn't make the leaving any easier. I just wanted to make the most of the time with her and stay as long as I could.

I was taken back to the children's home and stayed there during the daytime while the teachers decided what to do after the incident. I'm thankful that they didn't press charges against me for assault, but I soon found out that they'd decided I couldn't go back. I panicked, realising how school had been somewhat of an escape for me at that time. I knew I wasn't going to cope well with the exclusion. I was in a cycle of 'kicking off' every day with the staff, which involved getting restrained, dragged around, locked in rooms, cutting my arms and running away. I felt like I was in a repetitive nightmare, and I didn't know when it would end.

The police were constantly being called into the home, and it got to a point where Social Services decided that something drastic needed to happen because 'this behaviour' couldn't carry on. They gave me an ultimatum. My first option was to go into a therapy-style secure unit, or the second option was to move to a boarding school in the Northwest of England.

It wasn't a difficult choice for me. I love to learn, so boarding school was definitely my preference of the two. However, at the time of choosing, I didn't realise that the school was predominantly for children with emotional and behavioural difficulties. I often laugh when I look back now and think about the concept of putting a large number of children with behavioural challenges all in the same place in the middle of the countryside. Safe to say we had some 'interesting' times.

CHAPTER 3: TURBULENT TEENS

I had a wide range of experiences at the boarding school. I have lots of good memories of the time I spent there. We had masses of extra-curricular activities, which were fun and adventurous. We'd play hours of football, go on day trips to beautiful places, and I thoroughly enjoyed the trampolining competition experiences. We even went to a nearby retirement home to sing songs for the elderly residents. There were some truly beautiful moments.

There was a huge sports hall with trampolines, badminton and archery. There was a large open field with enough space for eleven-a-side football matches and go-karting. We even had access to motorbikes and a car to learn the basics of how to drive. There were classrooms filled with design and technology equipment, science apparatus and art supplies. I got on well with most of the teachers, and some of the time, I felt encouraged and supported by the staff team.

One of the main challenges I faced there was the environment. I wasn't oblivious to the fact that I had some 'behavioural and emotional' challenges, but some of the other children, I felt, were on a whole other level.

Trigger Warning – Self-harm

It wasn't long after arriving at the school that I began to make friends with some of the other children. Late one evening, another girl and I decided we didn't want to go to bed. We started being silly and barricaded ourselves in a bedroom so the staff couldn't get in. It rapidly turned from innocent fun to something dark and sinister when the girl I was with smashed a mug and started to cut her arms with it. I stood there in shock for a few seconds, wondering how it had escalated to that. I'd never witnessed someone else cutting themself before, and it certainly wasn't something I was expecting to see that evening. Up to that point, I'd only ever inflicted superficial scratches on my arms. But that night, she taught me how to self-harm more severely. I accidentally cut too deeply and started to cry and panic as I saw the blood trickling down my arm. I shouted to the staff, who were sitting in the corridor, telling them what had happened. They asked me to move the items that were blocking the doorway so they could come in and help. I moved the stuff as quickly as I could, and the staff came in to look at what had happened. They took me to the local hospital to get the cuts looked at, and a kind nurse cleaned and stitched up the wounds to allow them to heal properly. Although it was a scary experience for me, I also recognised how the staff showed me a deep level of emotional care and concern. So, for the rest of my teenage years, I used self-harm as a coping mechanism to get attention and time with the adults in my life.

Disclaimer Any form of self-harm should be taken seriously, whether it's deemed 'superficial' or 'severe'.

At times, it felt as though I was in competition with the other children, fighting for the attention of the staff and going to great lengths to get it. Other girls would pierce their ears and lips, so I did it too. They would self-harm to the point that they need stitches. I copied that, too. We would have competitions to see who could go the longest without eating food, to see who could be the thinnest, the fastest, the naughtiest. Engaging in those sorts of behaviours led to years of unhealthy thought and behavioural patterns for me, patterns that I've had to work exceptionally hard to unlearn and break free from as an adult.

I'd often do well in class and get 'good points' on the points system for behaviour. I enjoyed being told how well I was doing, so it was a little bit of an incentive for me. I did, however, notice that whenever I didn't get the points I expected, I would feel angry with myself and kick off in the classroom. I'd say things like, 'What's the point in me trying if I've messed up now, anyway?!' The staff sometimes helped me to rationalise and calm down enough to pull it back, but internally, I'd already started beating myself up. I recognise now that the way I was reacting was related to the way I was treated in a foster home as a small child. Whenever I didn't do things to an acceptable standard, the foster carers would hit me. So, as a teenager, instead of others hitting me for not doing well enough, I would verbally (and sometimes physically) beat myself up.

Much of the school day seemed to be structured around food. It was good in that I had lots of healthy options and choices, but I often chose the foods that would give me instant gratification. Aged 14, after years of being bullied about my weight, I started to suffer from an eating disorder. Sometimes, I would binge and make myself sick, and other times, I would obsess about calories and over-exercise to burn off whatever I'd eaten. I struggled with that pattern of disordered eating for around six years (I'll mention a little more about that later in the book).

One of the things I really enjoyed about the boarding school was the structure on Fridays. We'd only have half a day of classes, and in the afternoon, we could choose an activity to do. I almost always chose football. I loved the feeling of the wind blowing through my hair as I ran, the adrenaline rush of smashing the ball into the back of the net whilst a team of people cheered me on. I often received awards for 'Top Goal Scorer' and 'Player of the Match' and felt a sense of achievement when I took them home to show my mum.

When I'd lived at the school for a few months, I was allowed to have some home visits at weekends. I really looked forward to those times because I got to spend time with my mum and also because it meant I could have a break from school. Sometimes, my mum would cancel at the last minute, and it would send me into a spiral of negative emotions and behaviour. I used to think she cancelled on purpose because she didn't want me or she didn't care about me, but I realise now it wasn't because of me at all and that she had severe mental health difficulties and sometimes struggled to be around others.

I'm always amazed when I think back about how much inner and outer chaos I was managing as a teenager, yet I still achieved nine A-C GCSEs. I remember crying in most of my exams because of how stressed and pressured I felt. But I'm thankful that many teachers and support staff believed in me and did their best to encourage me in the process.

After I'd finished my GCSEs, I applied to a residential college, but my application was unsuccessful. Staying at the boarding school wasn't an option if I wasn't in higher education, so I had to find somewhere new to live — again! I had no idea where I was going to go. In desperation, I contacted a previous foster carer to see if she still looked after children. I explained the situation and was super excited when she said I could move in with her in a few days once she'd sorted out the paperwork with Social Services.

In July 2009, I moved in with a lady who used to foster me. I lasted about two weeks at her house before the placement broke down. She had changed a lot and was very strict. At that time, I was a very traumatised teenager with huge trust and authority issues. It was not a good match. I moved in with my mum for a week or so until my social worker found me a new place to live. The only option at that point was another children's home.

I was 16 when I moved in, and not long after arriving, I was introduced to a lady called Lucy, who was volunteering as an Independent Visitor. It was nice to have someone involved who was separate from the children's home, a person I felt comfortable talking to and going out with. I really enjoyed my time with Lucy. We'd go out on day trips together to festivals, nice restaurants, the theatre, etc. There were a few times when I struggled with my mental health, and Lucy didn't always know what to do to help. But she kept showing up. She didn't run away when I was displaying 'challenging' behaviours, and that's one of the ways she helped me. She chose to stay, even though it might have been easier for her to walk away.

Around the same time, I was also allocated a leaving care worker named Sam. I seemed to get on well with her straight away, and I found her caring and supportive. Again, she didn't always understand the behaviours I displayed, but she supported me as best she could. I'm thankful I had her and Lucy to help me with the journey into adulthood.

The leaving care team asked if I'd like to learn how to deliver training days to Social Work students as a person with lived experience of the care system. I jumped at the opportunity! I've always had a passion and desire to use what I've gone through for good, and this felt like a great place to start. I got trained up and was soon doing sessions with a local university on an ad hoc basis.

Some days, I struggled to motivate myself to get up and out of the children's home. I'd regularly hang around with the other children I lived with and other teenagers in the local neighbourhood. We'd binge drink, sleep with guys and smoke weed, thinking it was 'cool'. It wasn't. Part of me knew those behaviours were risky, but at that time, I honestly didn't feel like I cared. I didn't think anyone else loved or cared about me, so I didn't see the point in loving or caring about myself.

One night, I went out with a girl from the home, and we bumped into an older guy who I thought was her mate. We walked for a bit, then arrived at a patch of grass, where he told us to wait for him. Subconsciously, I thought, '*I'm not alone with the guy, so nothing bad's going to happen.*' I was wrong.

TRIGGER WARNING – SEXUAL ASSAULT/SUICIDE ATTEMPT

After a short time, the guy came back with two bottles of alcohol. I downed a bottle, and so did the other girl as we carried on walking the streets with the man. The alcohol quickly hit me, and the next thing I knew, we were walking through a park. I was so drunk I could barely walk, but I remember the guy telling my friend to leave us alone for a while. The sky and the ground felt like they were spinning as I lay on the cold, damp grass, and the guy started to take advantage of me. I wondered why I wasn't screaming, why I wasn't saying no and where my friend had gone. I don't know how long we were there, but when he'd finished what he was doing, he walked me to the park exit, where my friend was waiting for me. He quickly left, and my friend and I stumbled back to the children's home to get some sleep.

The following morning, when I woke up, I felt disgusting and dirty. I spoke to the staff about what had happened, and the police came to have a more in-depth conversation with me. I told them as much as I could remember about the previous evening, but I didn't get the response I was expecting. They told me that they couldn't arrest the man without any evidence, that they couldn't prove whether I'd said yes or no, and that it would be his word against mine in a trial. I couldn't quite believe what I was hearing! I felt so overwhelmed with anger and disgust that I contemplated how to end my life that day.

I ran out of the children's home and walked to a nearby motorway bridge. I peered over the edge, watching the cars whizzing by. As I climbed and stood on the metal railing, my thoughts were racing. I contemplated the pros and cons of jumping. I thought about my mum and brothers and how much they would miss me if I were gone. I felt more overwhelmed by the tormenting thoughts in that moment, as I hated myself for even thinking of doing such a thing to them. I leaned further forward, and just as I did, a police van pulled up beside me.

At the time, I was annoyed they'd been there to stop me from jumping, but now I see it as God's grace and faithfulness keeping me from a premature death.

The police took me back to the home, and for the twelve months following that incident, I dabbled with cannabis and consumed large quantities of alcohol in an attempt to forget what had happened to me. I was aged 17 at this point, but I was still very much a scared little girl inside. I put on a strong and obnoxious front, but internally, I was broken and desperate for love.

I would often stand outside the shops, asking strangers if they'd get some alcohol for me. One evening, I heard a man shout my name. I turned around to see a familiar face behind the wheel of his car. It was John! A member of staff from a previous children's home. We had gotten on well as I was growing up, and he had always stuck up for me when others tried writing me off as a 'naughty kid'. It was lovely to bump into him after such a long time. We stayed in touch, and I soon met his wife Ann and his daughter. They took me under their wing for a time and called me 'Daughter Number 4'. They were very much like family to me. I saw them as a gift from God, and they journeyed through some painful things with me, and I with them. They truly were a great support to me.

It was fast approaching my time to leave the care system, so Lucy and Sam started to look at different accommodation options with me. There were a few options, including supported lodgings, my own flat or supported mental health housing. I preferred the idea of sharing a house with another adult, as it felt like the only option that was similar to a family setting. At that time, I outright feared the thought of living on my own. Social Services were keen to help me transition well from one place to another, as my mental health was understandably rocky at that stage. They found a supported lodgings 'match', and I was surprised when they said that it was a man. I was told that I didn't need to fear any wrong motives because he was gay, but that wasn't much reassurance for me. He'd never supported teenagers before, and it soon came to light that he was doing supported lodgings as a 'stepping stone' to become a foster carer of young children.

One night, I went into the kitchen and saw him drinking with another guy. They were also sniffing cocaine. The other man asked me if I'd like to try some, and I gave him a look of disgust before saying no and heading upstairs to get away from the situation. I told one of the other girls in the children's home what had happened, and when we had a fallout, she told the staff. I was so annoyed and upset with her at the time. But now, I'm actually thankful for what she did.

With that placement breaking down, it meant I only had a few short weeks to find somewhere else to live before the care order I was under ended on my 18th birthday!

CHAPTER 4: FROM DARKNESS TO LIGHT

A lady from the council rang me to ask if I wanted to get involved in a service-user-led council group. I held back tears as I explained what had recently happened and how I needed to find somewhere new to live. She recommended a lady called Mariana, who also did supported lodgings. I called Sam (my leaving-care worker) to ask if this was a possibility, and to my surprise, she said yes. I visited two ladies who had spaces available, but I decided to move in with Mariana. I laugh about it now, but I didn't know at the time that the two ladies knew each other and were friends who attended the same church in Greater Manchester. So whichever lady I had chosen to move in with, God clearly had a plan to pull me out of darkness and bring me into His marvellous light (1 Peter 2:9).

But you are a chosen people, a royal priesthood, a holy nation, God's special possession, that you may declare the praises of Him who called you out of darkness into His wonderful light.

1 Peter 2: 9 (NIV)

On my 18th birthday, I unloaded my belongings with great trepidation into Mariana's house. She often talks about that day, as I was all 'dolled' up and ready to go out with friends for the night. How I managed to do that, amongst the overwhelming emotions and logistics of unpacking, was beyond me. But I did it. I felt anxious about moving into this new place, wondering if it would fall apart like countless other placements had in the past. I was pleasantly surprised when I instantly felt welcomed and loved. I felt a sense of contentment that surpassed all understanding, and I just knew that I was in the right place at the right time.

Mariana encouraged me to go to church with her to see if it would help with the depression I was feeling. I often responded with a flippant, 'Yeah, maybe sometime', not really intending to take her up on the offer.

Although for many months I battled daily with thoughts of suicide and self-harm, I still managed to begin a Level 3 apprenticeship in Business Administration. I was working with the local council, which meant I often bumped into staff from the children's homes I used to live in. Their faces were an absolute picture when they saw me sitting behind a desk in the same office as them. I remember seeing one of them struggling to get into the building because his fob was broken, and I seemed to be the only person who noticed. I briefly contemplated putting my head down and acting as though I hadn't seen him, before actively choosing to get up and open the door for him. His face looked full of shock and horror as he cautiously asked me what I was doing there. 'I work here', I replied, with a smile on my face. He walked away sheepishly, and I knew I had done the right thing in choosing compassion over revenge.

I attended the apprenticeship as often as I could, but I was regularly mentally unwell for weeks at a time. I had a few good friends at work who prayed for and encouraged me, along with Mariana, and I believe that helped carry me through that season. I was so broken and fragmented that no matter how much love and care Mariana and others showed me at that time, it just never quite felt enough. I wanted so much more from those around me, more than was humanly possible, and so I spiralled out of control as I sought more comfort and attachment in the wrong places. I know now that a lot of what I was seeking from people were things that could only be fully found in relationship with God, the One who created me and knows me intimately inside and out.

When I was too unwell to work, I spent most of my time alone in my bedroom, dwelling on the past and thinking about how unfair the world felt. I'd been struggling for many years with disordered eating, but it was particularly difficult for the first two years after leaving the care system. The thing about an eating disorder is that your mind convinces you that you're in control of it. But when I recognised the severity of the compulsive thoughts I was having around calories and weight loss, I knew I was very unwell with an eating disorder. I'd often beat myself up internally when I didn't reach the unrealistic weight loss goals I'd set for myself. I felt overwhelmed with feelings of guilt and disgust whenever I ate certain foods or hadn't managed to burn off the calories I'd consumed that day. At that time, my mind was telling me that I'd be happier and more beautiful if I was slimmer. But now I know that happiness and beauty are based on more than what shape or size your body is. And I am, in fact, fearfully and wonderfully made because God says so.

I was struggling so much with depression at that time that I was having thoughts that the world would be a better place without me in it. I felt mentally tormented, and I just wanted to be free.

Trigger Warning – Suicide attempt

On a cold, wet day in January 2012, I messaged Mariana and a friend from work. I told them how low I was feeling and apologised for all the pain I was convinced I'd been causing them. I felt like such a burden. I had the rope ready, tied it around my neck, and tied the other end to the bedpost. I prayed to God and said something like, 'If You're real, I need You to help me. I don't want to live like this anymore. Please change me and my life.' Then I lowered my body and slowly felt myself losing consciousness. I remember coming to and seeing a bright white light as a man kneeled in front of me. The police had cut me free from the bedpost and were shining the torch in my eyes to check for signs of life. I was taken to the hospital but released within a few hours. Not surprisingly, Mariana was in shock with the whole ordeal, and my relationship with her felt strained for a short time, but she continued to love and support me as best she could.

In February of that year, I went to church with Mariana. As I walked into the building, I felt overcome by a sense of peace and love. I surrendered my life and heart to Jesus and began to get to know Him. I attended Sunday school before services to learn more about God and was excited to join the praise and youth choir. I got baptised in July 2012 and noticed a difference in myself almost straight away. The baptism experience was not only invigorating, but also a monumental moment. I remember thinking that now I was a Christian, I wouldn't have struggles anymore. I learned relatively quickly that that's not exactly how it works! I began learning about the spiritual aspects of life and that there is still very much a battle going on. But one of the great things about being in relationship with God is knowing that I no longer face battles alone and I am victorious in Christ.

I started attending church regularly and began to make friends. I got on especially well with a girl called Sarah. She was only a couple of years younger than me, but she was kind and fun and also had a passion for singing (I'll share more about her later in the book).

There were so many people I got on well with at the new church, but there were two particular people I would often spend time with after Sunday services. Jasmine and Deborah (who are sisters) are the sort of people that you can easily see the light of Jesus shining through. Their hearts are so full of kindness and gentleness. We'd often sing and laugh together and enjoy the delicious Jamaican food they'd prepare each week for us to feast upon. I was still grappling with an eating disorder at that point, but they supported and encouraged me as best they could with it. I learned so much from them in that season of my life, and their consistency and support helped me more than they will ever fully know.

As I got to know God more, I started to recognise how much my life and I were changing for the better. I also knew there were a lot of things I needed to process and heal from. There was so much trauma from my past that was still impacting my perception of myself, others and the world at that time.

Amidst that realisation, a friend mentioned a six-month residential programme to me. She said it was a

Christian home based in the North of England. It was run by staff who were trained to support women who had struggles with mental health, substance abuse and eating disorders. I watched the online promo video and instantly knew this was somewhere I wanted to go. That very night, I filled out the application form, and in July 2013, I was accepted into the programme.

I didn't trust that the place was going to be safe, so I smuggled in a mobile phone to keep in touch with my mum (one of the rules was that phones were kept in the office). I was cautious and standoffish to begin with as I got to know the people there and the routine of the programme. One woman I clicked with straight away was Zarah. She was of a similar age to me, and she was full of fun and easy to chat with. We spent lots of our spare time in the home together, writing songs, taking pictures, and bouncing on the trampoline.

One of the things I noticed almost instantly about the home was the tangible presence of peace and love I felt there. The staff were supportive and loving, as were most of the residents. That isn't to say it was a walk in the park, though. The timetable and the rules were strict and regimented, and some days, I struggled with that. There were days when I felt depressed and didn't want to get out of bed, and it felt overwhelming having to force myself to do chores, go to classes and eat three healthy, balanced meals. I know now that the routine of the programme was for my good, but at the time, it was hard.

After about two weeks of being there, we went for the usual Friday outing. I snuck some money out at a cash point to buy and binge on sweets that afternoon. When we returned to the house later that evening, we sat down to watch a film. The film was quite disturbing. I went to seek support to help manage the emotions it had brought up for me, but the staff were helping another woman who'd also found the film distressing. Before I knew it, I'd walked out the door, through the gates and come across a small river. I contemplated jumping in but knew deep down it wouldn't achieve anything. A member of staff had followed me, speaking calmly whilst gradually edging closer to me. Eventually, she pulled me close and hugged me whilst I cried. I was an emotional wreck for the rest of that evening. I knew that because I'd left the premises, I'd be sent home for breaking the rules. I was desperately angry and disappointed with myself.

The following morning, the staff asked me to leave the programme. The despair I felt seemed too much to bear. I told them that I wouldn't last the six months they expected me to wait before reapplying to the residential home. They were sad to see me leave, but reiterated that I would have to wait six months to reapply unless God said otherwise. Thankfully, He did.

I stayed in contact with the staff whilst I bunked down at my mum's house, and within six weeks, I was back on the programme (this time without a smuggled phone). The next few months were truly transformational. It was amazing experiencing the love of God in more depth and having deep revelations of who I was created to be. I encountered the Lord's presence regularly and worked through many a challenge with Him and others. I got to know the voice of God for myself and was truly thankful for the opportunity to be in such a beautiful place whilst focusing on my recovery.

There were some exceptionally tough times, too. I had to face and acknowledge difficult things from my past. There were many days on the programme where my emotions were so overwhelming that I struggled to regulate them. I'm thankful that the staff and other residents continued to support and pray for me, even on those difficult days.

One of the amazing experiences I had at the home was when a prophetess from America came to spend the day with us. I was in awe of how accurately she heard God's voice, and most of the things she shared as a word from the Lord for me were spot on. I was very excited to know that things were going to get better for me and that the best was yet to come!

I didn't realise at the time of living in the residential home that I was struggling with a Dissociative

Disorder. In simple terms, I had compartmentalised parts of myself as a child as a way of numbing myself from the traumatic events of my childhood. It was a coping mechanism I used to survive my time in the care system. I see now how the setup of the six-month residential programme reminded me of the children's homes. The routine, the chores, the discipline. Many of the relationship dynamics happening there were triggering traumatic memories from my past. It was massively intense at points but also deeply healing. I can honestly say I felt relieved when they gave me a graduation and leaving date.

I got dolled up in a pretty pink dress and invited some friends to come and celebrate with me. The other residents and staff encouraged and prayed for me. They reminded me that this was just the start of my healing journey and encouraged me to 'not despise small beginnings'. I initially felt sad to leave the residential home because I'd had so many beautiful moments in that place, but the sadness soon turned to thankfulness when I thought of how much I'd experienced and learned. I also felt grateful for the fact that I could take these memories and tools I'd been given with me.

CHAPTER 5: OUT OF THE COMFORT ZONE

On my return to Manchester in April 2014, I moved in with my stepdad and mum for a few months. We'd enjoy pamper nights with mud masks and create an array of ice cream sundae concoctions. We'd often watch films together and spend hours chatting and laughing about random things. I cherished those moments with them both, as I thought about the time I'd lost with them in my childhood. I was thankful for the opportunity to feel and see restoration happening in my relationship with them.

Amazingly, the apprenticeship role with the council had been kept open for me. I returned to work and quickly realised that it was no longer a suitable workplace for me. I'd changed during my time on the residential programme, and I now had a deep desire to be in a place where I could grow and use my gifts, preferably alongside other Christians. So, I asked God for a new job opportunity.

Almost immediately, I received an email from someone mentioning a Christian organisation that was advertising a role for an intern! I filled out the application form and left the outcome in God's hands. It wasn't long before I received an interview date and made my way to the office to meet the staff there.

When I arrived, I was introduced to Fay (one of the leaders of the organisation). She came across as cool, calm, and collected. I knew from the way she carried herself that she had a deep relationship with God. I found this comforting and reassuring as Fay and the team led me through the interview questions. I was cautious about sharing everything from my past with them, but I equally wanted to be honest about some of the struggles I was still facing. Shortly after the interview finished, they told me that the decision was unanimous, and they all sensed God was saying to offer the job to me. I joyfully accepted their offer and was excited to start working with them. I was also very nervous. In the interview, there was talk of an upcoming mission trip to

Uganda that I was required to go on as their intern. I'd never even been on a plane before, so the idea of going all the way to Africa that year was terrifying.

In September 2014, I began the internship. As part of the role, accommodation was arranged for me, and I moved in with an elderly gentleman who was known to my colleagues. Things were running smoothly, to begin with, but it quickly dawned on me that I hadn't prepared myself for the challenges of working within a Christian ministry. I certainly hadn't thought through the difficulties I might face living with an elderly man who I didn't know. I felt extremely overwhelmed at points. As a way of managing the difficult feelings, I started using old coping mechanisms such as drinking and self-harm. I felt so disappointed in myself. My mind was telling me that I was back at square one, but I knew that was a lie. I had definitely healed and grown so much already. The recent difficulties I'd faced were helping raise awareness of the fact that a deeper level of healing was needed. It felt raw and painful at the time, but I never gave up on my relationship with God. Thankfully, He never gives up on me either. I know that God blessed me with that job and the community of people I was surrounded by, and in October 2014, we travelled as a team to Uganda.

Fay and Louise held my hand as we prepared for take-off. I was thankful that the first flight was a quick one, a connecting flight to Amsterdam. The next leg of the journey wasn't as swift and took what felt like an age. But I kept myself entertained by playing games and watching films on the built-in TV screen on the seat in front. After ten or so hours, we finally landed in Uganda. I was in awe of the fact that I'd managed to fly all the way from England to Africa. What an achievement!

I waited eagerly to get off the plane, not knowing what to expect. I imagined it would be cool as it was dark outside, but I was pleasantly surprised when the door swung open, and I was hit in the face with what

I could only describe as a wave of hot, sandy air. We hauled our luggage through the airport and scrambled into a van as we made our way to the accommodation.

The journey through Banana Village was extraordinary. It felt surreal as we drove through the streets that were swarming with people enjoying the nightlife. I found the soft hum of crickets chirping brought me great comfort, alongside sharing a room with Louise. I woke up the next morning to see what looked like two men sitting on the floor outside, playing an oversized board game. It wasn't until later that day, when the sun was shining, that I realised they were statues. I was amazed at the sight of monkeys roaming around the site freely. I was even more surprised when I came across a luxurious outdoor swimming pool! I felt blessed to be experiencing such amazing things.

I enjoyed many of the expeditions we went on. We went to churches and schools where we shared stories and gifts with the people we met. I also helped a lady paint a mural on a wall at a premature baby unit in a nearby hospital. We went for scenic boat rides along the River Nile and captured memorable photographs at the equator, admiring the natural beauty around us. It was as though my eyes were being opened to the realisation of how vast the world is. As amazing as that was, it was also a significant culture shock for me.

One evening, whilst out for dinner together as a team, a Ugandan man called me 'fat'. I was told that in Africa, being called fat is a compliment, but for someone who had just overcome an eating disorder, I certainly didn't see it that way! I was overwhelmed with flashbacks and difficult emotions for most of that trip to Uganda, and some nights, I used alcohol to try to block the overwhelm out. Fay and Louise often soothed me by singing and praying over me, but eventually, Fay told me that if I didn't stop drinking alcohol, then I'd have to go home early. The thought of going home alone on a plane from Uganda was enough to stop me from drinking for the rest of the time we were there, but I still had to find a way of managing the overwhelming emotions and flashbacks I was having. So, I was very dissociated and depressed for the rest of the trip. I was glad when the day came for us to head back to England.

When we returned to the UK, I assumed things would calm down for me mentally. Although I resumed healthy eating habits, I was very close to having a mental breakdown. I believe that if it wasn't for God providing Fay, Louise and others as a source of support at that time in my life, I would have likely ended up in hospital.

A meeting was held regarding the internship because of what had happened when we were in Uganda. However, I was pleased when they said I could continue working there with the proviso that I go to a residential rehabilitation home for a short time to get some help.

I searched online for residential places nearby and, within a week or two, moved into another Christian home. I knew instantly that I'd made a mistake. The rules were far too strict, and many of the other residents were withdrawing from drugs and/or alcohol. I felt very unsafe, and it wasn't a suitable place for me. I lasted about two weeks there before being asked to leave.

I sat at the bus stop with my belongings in bin bags. I cried as I came to the realisation that I wouldn't be able to continue with the internship and therefore didn't have accommodation either. I had to find somewhere new to live, again. I started having overwhelming emotions and flashbacks of the innumerable placements from the past that I'd been forced or asked to leave because of the breakdown of relationships. I could sense anger rising within as negative thoughts raced through my mind. I felt a cloud of despair and hopelessness looming over me as I questioned how I'd got myself into such a state again. In that moment, I thought, '*I'll call John and Ann. I know they'll come and help me.*' I knew I could count on them to be there when I needed them. I'm thankful to God for that. They came straight away and gave me a lift to my mum's. They even stayed a while to check that I was OK before heading off home.

Here I was again, back at my mum's house, not knowing what I was going to do next. As much as I loved my mum and stepdad, I also found it extremely difficult to live with them. I had my own mental health struggles, and they had theirs. But the three of us living together under one roof was a battle — mentally, emotionally and spiritually. I was incredibly proud of them for giving up alcohol though, because it made the dynamics of living with them somewhat easier to manage. They had struggled with alcohol problems for over twenty years, but with Will (my stepdad) being poorly and just about surviving several heart attacks, they both decided it was best to stop drinking.

When I was staying with them, I remember Will getting mad at me for 'talking about all this God stuff'. He'd mock me, and at one point, had me by the scruff of the neck in a threatening manner. Looking back now, I recognise it for what it was. A spiritual battle. The mocking caused some tension in our relationship, but I was thrilled when he started noticing how much I'd changed, and he began asking questions about the Bible. I tried to answer his questions the best I could, but also encouraged him to read and discover things within it for himself. So he did.

A few weeks later, I vividly remember Will sitting at the table with the Bible in front of him. We got chatting, and he looked me square in the face and said, 'I'm starting to think I've been living my life the wrong way for the past fifty years.' I was astonished. What a drastic difference that was to the previous conversations we'd had about faith!

Not long after that chat, Will became severely ill. He was in and out of hospital after being diagnosed with a chronic lung condition, sleep apnoea and other health issues. Amidst the hospital visits, my friends and I continued to pray with and for Will. I was overjoyed to witness him taking Holy Communion and having regular visits from the hospital chaplain. Even though it was difficult to see him in such physical pain, it was beautiful to see him finding inner peace and rest. He'd found comfort in his new belief and felt assured that if he were to die at any moment, he would be with God in eternity, forever.

CHAPTER 6: ESCAPING TO THE EMERALD ISLE

My stepdad's health was rapidly deteriorating. I knew he was unwell, but I was shocked when the doctors gave us the news that he had a maximum of twelve months left to live. My mum broke down, demanding a second opinion. She wondered if they'd somehow accidentally switched the records and were talking about a different patient, but they hadn't.

As Will was in and out of hospital, I kept searching for somewhere I could go to get some help with my mental health. I discovered yet another residential home for women, this time in Northern Ireland. I carefully considered if I felt able to leave my parents during such trying circumstances, but I felt desperately unwell. I prayed, filled out the application form, and asked God to make it clear to me whether I should go or stay.

Only days later, someone from the home in Northern Ireland called to offer me a place in their programme. I just knew I had to go. I packed my things, hugged my parents goodbye and boarded the plane. The plane landed, and I was filled with anticipation for this new adventure. I made my way through the glorious countryside to the house on the hill, where I was greeted warmly by smiley staff members and residents. They gave me a tour of the house before helping me upstairs with my luggage. I was slightly surprised by how comfortable and at home I felt in this new place and country, but I was thankful to be settling in well and feeling content.

Part of the programme involved weekly, faith-based, one-to-one sessions. It felt a similar style to counselling, but each session was centred around my relationship with God. I worked through lots of painful memories with the support staff but like the other residential placements I'd been in, I wrestled with the strictness of the rules. I was given regular 'disciplines', which included things like cleaning windows and weeding the garden. It often triggered me to feel like a child in the care system again, and I found that exceptionally challenging.

Although I found those disciplining moments hard, I'm thankful there were plenty of joyful moments, too.

I'll never forget the night I was baptised in the Holy Spirit. We were at a church service, and I was amazed to learn that we can be filled and empowered right now with the Spirit of God and that it didn't just happen in the Bible. I prayed in my heart, asking God to please baptise me in His Spirit. A group of leaders prayed with those of us who had said we wanted to be baptised in the Spirit. One of the team members was a male. He brushed past my arm as they prayed, and in that moment, my mind was bombarded with reminders of abuse from men in the past. I sensed God telling me to surrender and focus on Him. I wrestled with the intensity of the flashback for a while as God gently asked me again to surrender to Him. I took a deep breath, a leap of faith and whispered, 'I surrender.'

Immediately, a euphoric sensation covered my entire being, inside and out. I would describe it as an intense awareness of peace and weightlessness. I fell to the ground in what felt like slow motion, as though I was floating and landing on a cloud. I felt a hand pressed against my chest (though there wasn't a physical person standing above me). I heard God say, 'I'm healing your heart.' I lay in awe on the floor for some time as I encountered God and allowed Him to minister to me. I don't know how long I lay there for that evening, but I know I could have quite happily stayed there for the rest of that night.

I assumed it was getting late when people started to vacate the building, and a staff member tapped me on my shoulder and helped me to my feet. We piled into the van to head back to the house, some of us laughing uncontrollably for the remainder of the journey. It was hilarious. We sat around the table for supper, praising and worshipping. I know now that I was encountering the Holy Spirit, and I loved it. It was better than any effect I'd had from drugs or alcohol, and I learned that night that absolutely nothing compares to the presence of God.

Whilst on the programme, I used the phone at weekends to keep in touch with friends and family. I would nearly always call my mum because I missed her so much. For years, she had told me she was on the fence about God and had trouble believing He was real because of the horrific things she had endured. We were on a call together when she randomly came out with, 'I've decided to come off the fence.' I was ecstatic! I led her through a salvation prayer, and I cried with joy as we celebrated the momentous decision she'd just made! There was a significant shift in her mood and outlook on life as she began to pray and be encouraged. Even my stepdad Will recognised the difference in her.

A few months into my time at the residential home, I received a call from my mum about Will's health. I didn't handle the news well that night and ended up having an angry outburst, which involved shouting and swearing at another resident. I knew that I'd broken a few of the house rules, so I can't say I was surprised when I was asked to leave the programme. Although I felt annoyed with myself for yet another placement breakdown, I also felt relieved at the idea of spending some time with my stepdad for what I didn't know then would be his final days of life. I believe that God works all things together for good — even our mistakes.

7th of February 2016

Will and I laughed together that night, doing the conga to the bedroom as he held onto me for stability. I was glad our relationship had been restored, and there was no longer any contention between us. In his final months, I even started to call him 'Dad'. I knew how much that meant to him. He'd been like a dad to me and my siblings since childhood, so it made sense when 'Dad' started flowing naturally out of my mouth in conversations with him.

One of the things Will hated most about being unwell was having to use a machine at night to help him breathe. He was stubborn and frequently refused to wear it. Mum and I would put it on him whilst he slept but he'd often just pull it off. That evening, I helped him into bed and told him I loved him before saying goodnight and leaving him to rest.

8TH OF FEBRUARY 2016

I woke up at around 9.30 am on that cold Monday morning. I headed to my parents' bedroom to get ready in front of the wardrobe that was covered with mirrors. I gave a smile of contentment as I saw my mum and Will, both sound asleep in the bed behind me. I could see Will wasn't wearing his oxygen mask, and I thought to myself, '*He's gonna die one of these days if he keeps refusing to wear it.*' I thought to go over and put his mask on for him, but for some reason, I didn't.

I left for my appointment and then headed over to my friend's house to hang out. I flopped myself dramatically onto the bed next to my friend, letting out a sigh of relief. My phone rang, but I didn't pick it up. 'It can wait,' I said flippantly as I nestled into the mattress and cushion beneath me. 'If it's important, they'll leave a message.' I heard the voicemail notification sound and begrudgingly rolled over to see who it was.

A missed call from my mum.

I'd only just left their house, so why was she calling me so soon?

As I began listening to her message, I could tell from the tone of her voice that something bad had happened.

TRIGGER WARNING – BEREAVEMENT

I was in shock as I heard the words, 'Will's dead. Can you come back?'

Almost instantly, my mind started replaying comments my mum had made in the past about killing herself if Will ever died.

I got to the flat as fast as I could. My mum was lying on the floor, holding tightly to my stepdad's body. I'd never seen a dead person before, and it was a very surreal experience. I remember my mum saying, 'Touch him; he's cold.' I didn't want to touch him, but I didn't want to upset my mum either. He didn't feel cold to me, but maybe it was because I was in shock. For a split second, I thought, '*Maybe I can pray him back to life? Like Jesus did.*' I did pray. But he didn't wake up. He just lay there, lifeless.

I thought back to that morning, questioning if I'd put Will's mask on, would he still be alive now? I must have said it aloud because the paramedics responded, saying that he'd definitely been gone for many hours. They reassured me that he'd likely passed away around 3 or 4 am that day. They also helped me to realise that if I had gone over to put his mask on, it would have been me who found him dead that morning.

The next few weeks were a blur of adrenaline and emotional instability as I tried to arrange Will's funeral. My mum was just about coping but wasn't in a fit state to help much with the planning. I'm thankful for the amazing friends who came alongside me to support me with it all. And within a couple of weeks, the funeral was arranged. I recorded a song at a local studio, and we played it at the crematorium during the service. Mum loved it and was sure Will would have, too. I can't deny that it was an exceptionally difficult day, but it was lovely to celebrate Will's life and all that he had been to us. It was nice to see my brother Liam there, too. He'd been in prison for a few years, so it was a blessing that he was able to attend at such short notice.

Liam was released from prison only a few days after the funeral. He looked impressed when my friend and I arrived to pick him up in a fancy SUV. The conversation was relatively light as we drove to drop him off at my mum's.

'Why have you brought him here? Can't he stay with you?' my mum asked in desperation. I had two choices: I could give in and look after my brother (as I had done for most of our childhood) or stand firm and say no. I chose to say no.

'It's not my responsibility to look after him, Mum,' I said assertively. That was a boundary I knew I had to put in place. I used to hate boundaries, but now I recognise the significance of them. I love my brother, but I knew I couldn't live with him. That wouldn't have been helpful for his mental health or mine.

Trigger Warning – Suicide attempt

I went back to my friend's house (the one I was staying with at that time), and within a few weeks, I received the call I'd been dreading.

The hospital informed me that my mum had attempted suicide and was in critical condition in the Intensive Care Unit. I knew she wouldn't cope now that Will was gone. She was co-dependent on him. And without him, she genuinely didn't see the point in life anymore.

I went to visit her in hospital. I wasn't prepared for how overwhelming it would be to see her with wires and drips attached to her motionless body. I expected her to look peaceful, as though she were sleeping. But to me, she looked almost dead. I fled out of the room, refusing to see her until she'd been brought out of the coma.

Some hours or even days passed before the nurses told me that my mum had come around. I looked at her with compassion, hoping that one day, she would be strong and filled with life again. I wasn't anticipating the first words that came out of her mouth.

She looked me in the eye and whispered, 'I don't have anything left to live for now that Will's gone.' I'm not sure she realised how difficult that was for a daughter to hear from her own mother's lips. I abruptly reminded her that she had four children as well and that just because Will was gone now, it didn't mean her life had to end. The anger must have been visible on my face as she said, 'You've never looked at me in that way before.'

I could understand on some level that what she was saying was coming from a deep place of grief. But it was also an incredibly difficult thing for me to hear. I found it helpful to remind myself just how unwell my mum was and that, deep down, I knew she loved me. The way she was behaving wasn't a personal attack on me. She was struggling to comprehend the loss of her soulmate.

She didn't know how to live without Will. I continued loving, encouraging and praying for my mum, hoping that someday she would be OK.

She stayed in the psychiatric ward for a while, continuing to make good progress before being discharged. When I saw how well she was doing and knew she had Liam supporting her at home, I decided I wanted to return to Northern Ireland. The women's residential programme didn't have a space available for me straight away but reassured me that it wouldn't be too long a wait. I desperately wanted to get out of Manchester at that point, so I flew to Belfast and stayed in temporary accommodation there whilst waiting for the women's home to contact me.

CHAPTER 7: LOVE, LOSS AND LAMENT

On Sunday 15th of May 2016 (my mum's birthday), I attended a church service in Northern Ireland. The guest speaker shared a story which led me to think about my brother Liam. He'd been struggling with drug and alcohol addiction for a while. I wondered if there was anything the church could do to support him. At the end of the service, I felt prompted to ask the pastor. I was stunned when he simply replied, 'Go to Manchester, bring him over here, and we'll see what we can do.'

I rang Liam to let him know what I was planning to do, and he started to cry. I was slightly concerned and asked him what was wrong. He'd been on a journey of discovering God for himself. He told me how he'd made a deal with God. I chuckled but was also intrigued to find out more. He said he'd told God that if He answered three of his prayers, then he'd believe in Him and would surrender his life to Jesus. He cried as he told me that my call with the offer of a fresh start in Northern Ireland was his third answered prayer. Now I understood his tears. Liam was in a state of awe as he began to comprehend not only the existence of God but also the reality that this same God had heard and answered his heart's cry.

On Monday 16th of May, I flew to Manchester and arrived at my mum's flat. She grinned from cheek to cheek when she saw me waiting in the doorway. It was a lovely evening. It was a blessing to visit my mum and celebrate her birthday, but it felt tough breaking the news to her that the next day, I would be flying back to Northern Ireland, and this time, Liam would be coming with me. He'd been staying with Mum since coming out of prison, so she'd grown used to having someone there with her. She initially looked sad, but her facial expressions softened when she realised the significance of this next step for Liam.

'Go over there and get saved,' she whispered to Liam before we headed out to the airport.

The next morning, we arrived in Belfast and headed to the church. Many people were preparing for a conference, and I was delighted when I saw my brother chatting and praying with a man at a nearby stall. My eyes filled with tears as I watched Liam surrender his heart and life to Jesus.

He looked at me and said, 'Sis, I can feel it.' I knew exactly what he meant. He was feeling God's presence; a tangible peace and love that he'd never properly experienced before. I was blessed to witness such a precious encounter.

Liam quickly made friends at the church in Northern Ireland. Meanwhile, I was pleasantly surprised to receive a call from the women's home about an available space for me. I accepted their invitation and packed my things up before taking the short car journey to the home. The transition felt smooth, and I started to feel settled. During my stay at the home, I'd often call and write to family and friends as a way of staying in touch with them. I especially enjoyed writing letters to Liam, even though he lived nearby. One day, I heard God asking me to send a letter to Liam, telling him that the Lord was giving him the new name David. Back then, I had little understanding of the significance of names or how to explain it to my brother. But I wrote the letter and sent it, anyway. On the next call with Liam, we chatted about the letter. To my amazement, it made complete sense to him. A few days before receiving my letter, Liam was standing outside and heard someone shouting the name 'David'. My brother asked the man he was staying with if he had heard the voice, but he hadn't. Liam said he went back outside and heard the name David being shouted again. So, when he received my letter, it resonated with him.

On Wednesday 29th of June 2016, I found out my mum had gone into hospital with agonising pain in her stomach. I wasn't overly concerned because she'd had it before, so I assumed it was a flare-up and she'd be feeling much better soon.

The following morning, I led a devotional session with other residents. I'd heard an encouraging message about the power of celebrating your victories (no matter how big or small) and how this can often help strengthen you for your next battle. I thought it was a cool concept. We wrote our victories on the board and sang and danced in celebration. It was great fun! I have no doubt that celebrating those victories that morning was great preparation for the battle I was about to face.

I asked to call my mum to check how she was doing. A staff member handed me the phone and joined me in a quiet room at the back of the house. The hospital clerk answered, seeming unsure of which ward to transfer my call to. They put me on hold multiple times, and I could feel myself becoming agitated with the length of time it was taking them to locate which ward my mum was in.

I assumed she'd been moved, and they were trying to figure out where, but it soon transpired that wasn't the case at all.

Trigger Warning – Bereavement

As the lady on the other end of the phone began to speak, I could tell from her tone that something had happened to my mum. She informed me that the police had been trying to contact me. I told her that I was in a residential home where I didn't have constant access to my mobile phone.

Without a word of warning, she said, 'I'm sorry. Your mum went into cardiac arrest, and she didn't make it.'

I threw the phone across the room and fell to the floor in shock. I heard myself screaming, repeating, 'No, no, no, no, no!' as I covered my face with my hands. For a second, I wondered if I'd made a mistake. *Maybe I'd heard her wrong?* I asked the staff to call her back, hoping that I'd misheard what she'd said. But it was confirmed again that my mum had passed away. I screamed and cried inconsolably on the floor for some time as a staff member hugged and held me. I remember needing some fresh air and shakily making my way outside to sit on the bench. I felt so angry with God, and shouted to Him, 'I thought You were going to restore the years that the locusts had eaten?'

I couldn't see at that time how that was going to be possible now that my mum was dead. But I distinctly heard God say to me, 'I am going to restore the years; it's just going to look different to how you expected.' I scoffed angrily at His response but was too numb to properly process what was going on. I went back indoors, and the other residents hugged me and said how sorry they were. I walked into the conservatory, turned on the CD player as loud as I could and blasted some worship music. I sang and felt comforted by God. Even though I felt angry with Him, I knew He was the only one who could properly comfort me in that moment.

An hour or so passed before the manager encouraged me to meet Liam to tell him the news. We got in the car, and she drove us to the church. I sat in stunned silence with Liam as he waited to hear what had happened. My eyes were red and puffy from crying, and I sat there sombrely as he asked me what was going on. Tears rolled down my cheeks as I desperately looked in the direction of the manager for some help. She gently nodded and recounted the events of that morning to Liam. As she told him, he looked at me in disbelief, crying and shouting angrily. He told the woman to leave us alone, and I hugged and held him tightly as we sobbed together.

I repeated 'I'm sorry' over and over, knowing exactly how he was feeling. I was apologising because I knew that we both had wanted our relationship with our mum to be better in adulthood than it was in our childhood years. We thought we'd have more time with her. But just like that, she was gone.

When Fay and Louise heard the news, they kindly offered for me to stay at their home whilst I organised the funeral. I felt relieved when the plane touched down in Manchester, and I headed over to visit my older brother Jacob to see how he was doing. Understandably, he'd been struggling with the loss, but it felt somewhat comforting as we hugged and cried together. We were surprised that within a few short days, my mum's landlord contacted us, saying that we needed to empty her flat so that someone else could move in. I couldn't quite believe how quickly they were expecting us to sort through her belongings. It felt very surreal and very distressing.

I woke up that morning, downed a bottle of vodka, and headed to Mum's flat to start the sorting process. The day was long and laborious, my judgement clouded by grief and drunkenness. As we sorted through Mum's belongings, keeping her 'stuff' felt meaningless to me. Jacob didn't feel the same way about it and wanted to keep quite a few of her things. But I didn't want to keep anything that would remind me of her. I guess that was my way of dealing with her death for the first few years. Everyone deals with grief differently.

My mum had tried to apply for life insurance before her death, but because she'd attempted suicide so many times and had significant medical problems, she was unable to find a company that would cover her. She hadn't exactly planned to die aged 45, so I know it wasn't her fault she didn't have savings or a funeral plan. But it did make the first few weeks following her death even more of a challenge. We'd only just finished paying for Will's funeral, and now we had to raise another £3,000 to cover the cost of our mum's. We had to sell some of her things, but I also set up a fundraising page. I was thankful so many people donated, making the process easier.

A few days before Mum's funeral, it was my 23rd birthday. I forced myself out with friends to 'celebrate', but I wasn't mentally present in the room with them. I sat at the table feeling numb and weary whilst others smiled and laughed, deeply engrossed in conversation. *How were they so happy? Had they forgotten that my mum had just died?* It was tough to see others seemingly getting on with life whilst, internally, I was screaming. One of the things about grief is that it feels as though you're stuck in a moment in time. A memory, a feeling, desperately holding on to the thing or person that you would love to still be there. The world carries on as normal whilst inwardly, you feel you're at a stand-still. It can be exhausting.

MUM'S FUNERAL AND CREMATION

Liam said he wasn't coming back to Manchester yet, and he wasn't up to coming to Mum's funeral. I tried to convince him otherwise, but I knew it was his way of dealing with the loss. I cried uncontrollably as the hearse pulled up outside my mum's flat. It suddenly felt very real. My auntie squeezed my hand tightly, reminding me she was right there beside me and that we would get through the day together. I wiped away the tears and climbed into the car. As we travelled, I imagined in my mind that we were a family reenacting a sorrowful scene from a film. As we entered the grounds of the crematorium, it was a stark reminder that this wasn't a film, we weren't actors, and this was actually happening. The coffin was gently lifted out of the hearse before being placed on the undertakers' shoulders and carried into the crematorium.

The service went as smoothly as I could have hoped for. Fay and Louise sang a song, and Fay led the ceremony beautifully. They played a song that I'd pre-recorded. A song I knew my mum would have loved. I didn't feel up to singing it live that day. I held myself together for most of the service but broke down in tears as they removed the coffin to prepare for the cremation. Logically, I knew it was only a body and that my mum's spirit was no longer there. Emotionally, it was tough. It was as though I were saying goodbye to her, only this time, I knew it was forever.

After the funeral, I planned to move back to Northern Ireland, but God had other plans. I chatted briefly with Louise and Fay about accommodation before heading to the shops to get them some 'thank you' gifts. When I returned, I gave them a candleholder in the shape of a house. It represented their house as being filled with light and love. I was elated when they told me they had a gift for me, too. They handed me a card that also had a picture of a house on it. Inside the card was a key to their home. They told me how, earlier that day, God had spoken to them about me. They felt led to let me move in with them and for their house to be like a home for me. I wondered if they were joking at first but quickly realised from the expressions on their faces that they were being serious. I eagerly accepted their offer and was excited when we started moving my belongings from the guest wing to the main living quarters of the house.

Whilst living with Fay and Louise, I often grappled with the concepts of 'family' and 'home'. I loved the idea of it because it's what I'd hoped for in my childhood, but there were moments when it felt overwhelming for me. I was grieving the death of my mother while learning what it was like to live in a family environment. There was so much happening all at once, but I was thankful to have somewhere stable to live at such a difficult point in my life.

For the first few months, I remember feeling desperately depressed. I drank most days in an attempt to blot out the pain, but it tended to exacerbate the situation. I'd often scream, 'I want my mum,' though I knew no amount of wailing or crying was going to bring her back. Others encouraged me to 'move on' and 'let go' of my mum. But at that time, it didn't feel that simple for me. I wasn't just grieving the death of my mum; I was grieving the childhood dreams I'd had of living with her and being close to her. It was an inner battle, coming to terms with the reality that my mum was going to be absent for the rest of my adult life, too.

Fay, Louise and countless others supported me the best they could through those difficult days and nights. I'm very thankful God blessed me with them for that season of my life. I know I wouldn't have gotten through it without them.

In August 2016, a friend and I planned a spontaneous trip to a Christian worship weekend in West Sussex. We packed some bags and jumped in the car before making the six-hour-long journey to a quaint little town called Shoreham-by-Sea. I didn't know what the weekend would entail, but I was pleasantly surprised. We set up camp near the main event tent and were blessed to hear the gentle sound of singing each night as we drifted off to sleep. It was an amazing experience. There was a chance to mix with other campers throughout the day, and I soon got chatting with a group of cheerful ladies who were camping next door to us. They encouraged and spoke to me about the name Esther, and I sensed God was speaking to me through those ladies.

When I returned home from the trip, I continued chatting with God about the name Esther. I knew it resonated with me. I sensed the Lord asking me to change my name, so I said to Him, 'If You want me to change my name, please can you show me a car with the initials EGJ on the registration plate?' For years, I'd really liked the idea of having a car with my name or initials on it, so although it seemed like a random thing to ask for confirmation through, God knew my heart in it. I went out for a ride on my bike, not thinking much about the prayer I'd just prayed. But as I cycled up the narrow path towards home, I looked up, and there it was! A car headed in the same direction with the letters EGJ on the registration plate. I felt goosebumps all over and sensed God confirming the new name He was giving to me. I had many confirmations over the coming weeks, and I gradually started asking people to call me Esther.

I had lots of wonderful experiences whilst living at the house with Fay and Louise. We'd regularly cook and eat together. We'd go for walks in areas with gloriously pretty landscapes and explore new places. Although there were plenty of lovely moments there, I often felt engulfed in a sea of loss and grief as I came to terms with the death of my mum.

CHAPTER 8: NEW BEGINNINGS

The weekend of my mum's first death anniversary, I drank heavily as I spiralled into a place of despair and despondency. I had an argument with others at the house before shouting and punching a wall in frustration. At that point, Louise and Fay said I needed to leave, and I could no longer live there with them. I sat on the floor crying before leaving in a drunken state. The level of overwhelm and distress I felt during that incident was inexpressible. Thoughts and images flashed through my mind of previous homes and relationships that had also gone so terribly wrong. I loathed myself in that moment, knowing that if I'd behaved differently, then I wouldn't have been asked to leave.

I called my friend Rae, who came to pick me up and said I could stay with her until I found a place of my own. I'd met Rae years earlier whilst doing an apprenticeship with the council, and her love and compassion shone through. She'd often been there for me at difficult times and was very much like a mum figure to me for a season.

Whilst living with Rae, I prayed daily. I asked God to show me what to do and where to go. I was technically classed as homeless at that point, so the local authority searched for suitable accommodation for me.

One day, I went past a college with a big sign saying, 'ENROL ON AN ADULT COURSE TODAY!' I enquired about which courses were available and chuckled when they told me that the only 'free course' I could apply for that day was an accounting one. I'd felt prompted earlier that year to start an accounting course, but for various reasons, I hadn't, so I knew it was the right next step for me. I enrolled immediately and began preparing myself mentally for the start date in September 2017.

The following day, the council contacted me regarding a supported accommodation flat in Greater Manchester. I viewed the property, signed some forms, and within a few days, I was ready to move in.

On my 24th birthday, I was still staying with Rae. I vividly remember her son waking me up, closely followed by Rae carrying a personalised birthday cake with balloons and party poppers. I smiled in appreciation, knowing they wanted to make my birthday extra special after the ordeal I'd just been through. I prayed and asked God what I should do that day and felt Him asking me to go to a prayer meeting. At first, I was like, *'Wait, what? A prayer meeting on my birthday?'* However, I've learned that being obedient to God is always a good thing. Not because He'll hurt or smite me if I don't obey Him, but because He's a loving Father, and He knows best.

I yawned and stretched before mustering up the strength to get ready and go to the prayer meeting. At the beginning of the session, I saw a lady who looked familiar. As we did a name round, I realised who she was. This lady had been my childhood dentist! She was very memorable to me as I'd bumped into her one time when I'd run away from the children's home. It was Christmas time, and I'd decided to knock on people's doors to sing some carols and make some money. I knocked on a door in the local village, and to my surprise, my dentist lived there. She listened to my Christmas carols before praying with me and contacting the children's home to let them know I was at her house. I was amazed that over ten years later, I was sitting in the same room with her at a Christian gathering. She started to cry as she told me she'd recently asked God to show her that her prayers were having an impact. And there I was, a lady she'd prayed for over ten years ago. It was a great encouragement to both of us, and I was thankful I'd listened to God's prompting to go to the meeting that day.

A few days later, I moved into the supported accommodation. I'd never lived on my own before, and for many years, I had a deep fear of it. But I settled in really well and was happy with how quickly the place began to feel homely.

I reconnected with Sarah around that sort of time, too. She lived a short walk away from my new place, and I was glad when we started hanging out again. She was one of the first friends I'd made at church, and she'd helped me feel accepted and loved. We've been good friends ever since.

She told me about a young adult's house group nearby, and I went with her to see if I liked it. They were a very welcoming bunch, and I found making friends there was relatively easy. I got on particularly well with Dot, Harper and Rebecca and became part of their friendship group for some years. They attended a different church to me, but that didn't seem to matter. I'd been praying for a group of friends my age, and this was a definite answer to my prayer. They were a significant blessing to my life and healing journey, and I thank God for them. They supported, prayed for and loved on me through some of the darkest and most difficult moments. Rebecca and Dot often invited me to family events and holiday celebrations, too. This was extremely healing for me, as I gained a deeper knowledge of that feeling of being part of a family.

Also in 2017, I took part in a ten-week prayer school. I got chatting with many amazing people, some of whom are still in my life today. It was there that I met Caleb and Flora. We became friends and met up regularly throughout the ten-week course. We'd laugh, eat, pray together, and had lots of fun moments. One of the things I was amazed by was how comfortable I felt around Caleb. Caleb was one of the first men I felt I could be alone with in a room and still feel safe. God used that situation to bring significant healing from the fear I had of men. I'm truly thankful for the opportunity to get to know such a loving and beautiful couple, and I don't think they knew how much of a blessing they were at that time.

During the prayer school, I also met the Smith family. Hope and Grace Smith were a similar age to me. They came across as really confident as they helped to lead some of the sessions. Their mum, Dee Smith, was also involved, coordinating refreshments and other bits and bobs. One of the first memories I have of meeting Dee was at the refreshments stand. I chatted with her briefly before giving her a big hug and heading home. Dee's hugs are amazing! Whenever she hugs me, I sense her mothering heart and instantly feel cosy and warm. It's such a powerful representation of the heart of God and how we're always safe and held in His arms.

You know when someone comes into your life, and you just know straight away that you were destined to meet? When you relate on such a level with someone, as though you've known each other for a lifetime? Well, Dee is one of those people for me. She has been and continues to be a good and faithful friend.

In early 2018, things were particularly difficult for me. I began my journey with therapy, as I knew it was time to start dealing with the deeper things that were going on for me internally. It wasn't an easy process. As I started the therapy sessions, it was as though I had opened a box that had been tightly shut for many, many years. I would frequently call Dee and her daughters in the midst of reliving painful memories through flashbacks and dissociative episodes. I hadn't realised until that moment that I'd not yet fully acknowledged, faced or known the depth of the trauma I had come through. My brain had managed to compartmentalise and store the traumatic memories away for so long, as though wanting me to remain oblivious and numb to those horrifying past events. But they were no longer hidden; the box had been opened.

I know God's Grace brought me through that difficult season. I also love how He's given us great capacity to be a source of encouragement, comfort, and strength to one another, too. I know for a fact I wouldn't be where I am today without the input I've had from others. I thank the Lord for my relationship with Him but also for those He's blessed and blesses me to do this journey of life with.

CHAPTER 9: FACING THE TRAUMA

My relationship with my brothers has been significant, too. I've journeyed through many difficulties with them, and they have, at times, been a great source of comfort and support. In early 2018, my brother Jacob and I were chatting on the phone about some awesome dreams I was having. He sounded disappointed as he told me that he rarely had dreams, and if he did, he didn't particularly remember them. So, I prayed with him and believed that he would have a dream very soon. The next time we spoke, he excitedly told me about a dream he'd not only had but remembered! He said that in the dream, he was on a cross next to Jesus, and Jesus was telling him how much He loves him. I was amazed at how rapidly the prayer had been answered.

And secretly, I think Jacob was, too. Not long after that dream, Jacob came to church with me. There was an opportunity at the end of the service for those who wanted to surrender their lives to God to raise their hands. I was delighted to see my big brother lift his hand and repeat the salvation prayer. It's a moment I will always cherish. It was beautiful to witness my brother experiencing the presence of God. And for the first time in a very long time, he looked at peace.

Soon after that, my younger brother Liam came back to live in England. He wasn't coping well with Mum's death and had started struggling with drink and drugs again. I managed to contact a Christian rehab for him, and he moved in relatively quickly. One of the challenging things about Liam's housing situation was that he'd gotten into a pattern of staying somewhere for a maximum of twelve months before walking out or kicking off. I could empathise with that situation. It was extremely difficult to watch, but I'm sure it was even harder for him to be experiencing it. I continued to support him the best I could and helped him get into lots of different accommodations, but he'd repeat the same cycle again and again.

I realised after months of therapy that there was very much a 'mother' and 'child' dynamic at play in the relationship with me and Liam. That way of relating with my brother had gone on for so long that I knew it wasn't going to be an easy thing to change. I tried to exert better boundaries with him, but this often led to verbal altercations. Whenever I helped him, it was detrimental to my mental health, and it would take me weeks to recover. I love Liam very much but I realise now that I wasn't well enough to support him in the way that he wanted or needed. For years, I felt guilty about that, but I've let that guilt go now. I know that I love my brothers. I know that I do the best I can with them. And I believe that deep down, they know that, too.

In the summer of 2018, I ventured to the Christian worship weekend in West Sussex (the same event I'd attended in 2016). I volunteered on the team to gain some experience of what it would be like as a team member at a big event. I enjoyed most of what went on that weekend, but I wasn't best pleased when a storm broke out and the tent I was staying in leaked and fell apart. I was soaked, my clothes were soaked, and quite frankly, I felt like crying. I trudged through the wet field to dry off in the team tent. I took a deep breath and slumped onto the sofa before removing my shoes to let my socks dry out. A little girl came bounding up to me, smiling and joyful. She was extremely chatty, and her family soon came over to join in the conversation, too. The mum (Wendy) was a beautiful lady with a newborn baby boy attached to her side. The dad (Peter) was friendly and approachable, and they had an older daughter, who surprised me with how unbelievably clever she was. I had a great time getting to know them, and as we exchanged numbers before leaving the event, I didn't know how much of a blessing these new friends would be. I've been friends with Peter and Wendy and their children for quite some time now. It's amazing how the seemingly awful situation of the tent leaking rapidly turned into a wonderful moment that brought about new friendships.

I arrived home in August and felt led to start a Theology (Youth and Community) degree at a local university. I went to an open day on campus to hear more about the course and knew straight away it was something I wanted to do, so I signed up there and then.

The first few orientation classes were held over a weekend. They did it that way to give us an opportunity to get to know other students and to gain a deeper understanding of what the next few years of study would look like. I found the group an interesting bunch. There was one lady with whom I got chatting, and within a few seconds, I knew we would be good friends. Melisa came across as shy and reserved when we first met. But the more I got to know her, the more I realised she definitely was not shy. She has such a beautiful heart, and the kindness and gentleness of Jesus shine through her.

We became friends almost instantly (as I'd guessed we would), and during our time studying at university, we were seldom seen on campus without one another. We laughed together, sang together, studied together, ate together, and, on occasion, arrived late for class together — oops! I genuinely believe that if she hadn't been on the course at the same time as I was, I wouldn't have stayed there as long as I did. I am so thankful for her and our friendship, and I see it as a gift from God.

During the first week of university, I took part in an intensive week. The structure condensed a unit of classes typically spread out over two-hour sessions each week into a five-day period. The word intensive was very fitting! I felt like quitting on the first day, but instead, went for a walk in the nearby village. It felt very surreal. They were the same streets I'd walked along as a child when I was going through abuse and trauma. I prayed as I strolled down the familiar cobbled streets. I sensed a strong awareness of God's presence with me, bringing healing to the wounds and the memories. It was a profound and beautiful experience. As I walked past a tree, I saw some white plastic bottles that had pictures of a dove on them. The dove in Christianity is often a symbolic reminder of the Holy Spirit. I went all tingly as I sensed God reminding me of how far He'd brought me since my childhood. There was such peace surrounding me, and I felt noticeably lighter, as if a weight had been lifted. This encounter strengthened me and helped me continue studying at university.

As I began the university course, I noticed how difficult I found it to concentrate in class. I was also struggling to finish assignments on time. I was still having weekly therapy sessions and realised that working through childhood trauma isn't a straightforward process. There were times when I felt ridiculously overwhelmed, which was exacerbated when I believed the lies that my friends were too busy to support and be there for me. I even grappled with my faith in God. I'm thankful that God isn't fazed by doubts and questions. He doesn't up and leave when I'm questioning, angry or upset that things didn't quite turn out the way I thought they would. He waits, listens, embraces me and encourages me with the truth. I know that I have many good friends who support me, too, but that wasn't always easy to see in the midst of processing traumatic memories. It wasn't always easy to distinguish the difference between the feelings from 'back then' to the present-day reality.

Some people would say, 'Just forget about what happened in your past; you're not there anymore.' As much as I agree with not living in your past, if there are things in your history that are still negatively impacting the way you live in the present, then it's not quite as simple as just forgetting it happened. I tried for years to suppress the memories from my childhood, to just forget about them, but there came a day when that was no longer an option anymore, and I had to face and deal with the trauma.

A short time into studying for my degree, a friend invited me to her church to see her sing in the choir. I woke up late that Sunday and contemplated not going. I felt it was important for me to go because I'd told her that I would, so I got ready as quickly as possible before ordering a taxi and rushing out of the house. As I arrived at the church, I remembered I didn't have cash on me, so I briskly ran to a nearby shop. As I approached the cash point, someone was sitting beneath it. To my surprise, it was my younger brother! I withdrew some cash before helping him up and saying, 'Come on, we're going to church.'

As we made our way through the auditorium, the man who was preaching said, 'David, you are loved. David, you are important' and other statements beginning with the name David. My brother and I looked at each other in complete amazement, as we knew God was speaking directly to my brother through this man. As you read earlier in the book, God had spoken to us both about the new name David.

After my friend sang and the service ended, my brother and I went out for food together. I gave him some money and a phone charger, so he could at least stay in contact with people. I sensed myself going into the 'mother' role and hastily agreed for him to spend the night at my place. The next morning, we went to the town hall, and I helped him to get temporary accommodation. He stayed there for a few months before he became homeless again.

Towards the end of that year, I attended a prophetic conference organised by Freshfire Church. I was elated when I bumped into the same prophetess who'd visited the women's residential home in 2013. I looked around the room in awe of how passionate and engaged the people at the conference were. I felt intrigued by this new church and the healing ministry that they had. I knew I wanted and needed more healing, so it made sense to me when I felt led to start attending Freshfire Church regularly.

CHAPTER 10: LOCKDOWNS AND LOCKUPS

I started going to Freshfire Church properly in early 2019. I quickly settled in and became part of the family. One of the things I instantly loved about Freshfire was that I felt able to be myself without feeling judged or ostracised. For the first few months, I struggled massively with dissociative episodes. I believe that some of those behaviours were coming up because God was healing me more deeply from the trauma and pain of the past. Also, I felt safe enough to express what was going on with me. It wasn't an easy process for myself or those around me. But I'm thankful it happened. I got chatting with a lady called Kate about the healing ministry (Restoration Centre) that had been mentioned at the conference, and I soon booked a time to meet with her and another lady called Rosemary.

I met with them both to have some prayer ministry sessions. The aim of the sessions was to allow God into any wounded and hurting places for Him to shed light and bring healing. The sessions were Holy Spirit-led, and often, I would have deep times of encounter with God. I'd have pictures and visions in which I heard Him speaking good and beautiful things to and over me. I'm massively thankful that I have encounters with God outside of the Restoration Centre sessions, too, but it was extremely helpful at that time to have people alongside me to help facilitate those encounters when I was struggling to engage with God intimately for myself. I soon started to spend time with Rosemary outside of sessions, too. She'd often invite me over for tea, and sometimes, I'd sleep over at her house. She felt very much like a mum to me in that season, and God used her mightily to bring some healing from mother wounds from my past.

Another restorative experience happened in February of that year when I found out my biological dad had died. I know it sounds strange to label such a situation as restorative, but let me explain.

The news hit me pretty hard, and I was surprised by the amount of tears I cried. It's not that I didn't love my dad; I really did. I just didn't know him. I knew that the tears were related to grieving not only the loss of him but also the expectation I had that we'd get to know each other more in adult life. I didn't expect him to be gone so soon. The beautiful part of this story, though, is that a year or so before my dad's death, I had (for the first time) called him to wish him a happy Father's Day. I know it meant a lot to him. I wanted to honour the fact that he was my dad, even if he hadn't always made the best decisions. I'm thankful I listened to the prompt to call him because now I can say that one of the final conversations I had with him was one of restoration. Thank you, Jesus.

Around that time, I also got chatting with a lady called Carolyn. Carolyn had been through abuse as a child and had used dissociation as a coping mechanism. When I met her, she shared her story of healing from Dissociative Identity Disorder, and I was inspired by how she was using what she'd been through to help equip others. She sat down with me and a few friends to set up what she calls a 'truth team'. The idea of the truth team was that each member would commit to a certain role. Each role incorporated practical and emotional ways of supporting me, both regularly and consistently. (You can read more about how to set up a truth team in Carolyn Bramhall's book, 'Intelligent Loving'.)

I often had sleepovers with friends on the team, and others invested in my life in different ways. I'm so grateful for the hours of care and compassion they showed me throughout that season. It felt as though the team were holding me up on days when I felt I couldn't do it for myself. I no longer have the structure of a truth team, but I do have friends and church family who I do life with and am very thankful for.

In September 2019, I moved from the supported accommodation into a housing association property. My aunt helped me deep clean the place, and some friends generously donated pieces of furniture and household items. It soon started to look and feel homely, and I began to feel settled there. However, not long after moving to that property, I noticed that it often smelled of cannabis. The nights that I slept there, I'd wake up in a panicked state as the smell triggered flashbacks from the negative experiences I had with cannabis as a teenager. One particular night, I felt so triggered that I grabbed my sleeping bag and headed outdoors to sleep under a tree. It's crazy that I felt so anxious in that place that sleeping outside seemed like a safer option to me. I reported the issue to the landlord frequently, but there wasn't technically anything they could do to stop the smell or the neighbours from smoking cannabis indoors. So, I prayed desperately for a resolution because I knew I couldn't continue living there if the issue wasn't resolved.

THE PANDEMIC

March 2020 was an incredibly strange month.

There was talk of a virus that had started to spread around the globe, with not much explanation or understanding of what it was and how it would affect those who caught it. It soon came to light that lots of people were dying from it. There was mention of an upcoming lockdown, and I started to panic, as the thought of being forced to stay in a cannabis-stinking flat for an unknown length of time felt unbearable. I contacted my friend Jane and asked if I could stay with her if there was a lockdown. She graciously agreed, and on the 23rd of March 2020, the UK officially went into lockdown, and I temporarily moved in with Jane and her son, Danny.

It felt strange to be forced to stay indoors. We were permitted to leave the house for an hour a day (to exercise) and could only make trips to the local shops for essentials. We were also told to wear facemasks and keep at least 2 metres from others. It was so weird. For months, I felt overly anxious whenever I touched anything. I stocked up on hand sanitiser, and whenever I touched a door handle or an item that had been outside, I would have a strong compulsion to wash my hands immediately. I thought watching the news would help ease the anxiety I was feeling, but the media mostly just shared statistics of the rising number of hospitalisations and deaths. I decided it was best for me to stop watching the news for a while. It's not like I was oblivious to what was going on because everyone was talking about the pandemic anyway, but choosing to limit the time I spent focusing on the virus was a helpful coping strategy for me.

One of the things I did enjoy about the first lockdown was the weather! The sun shone gloriously almost every day. When we went for walks, it was beautiful, almost as though we were on a prolonged summer vacation. For that, I was truly appreciative. One of the downsides to the lockdown, though, was how it significantly impacted the mental health of many. My brother Jacob was one of the people who found it exceptionally difficult.

It was evening in early April 2020, and I sent a simple good night message to Jacob before bed. His response was only slightly different than usual, but from it, I could tell that something wasn't quite right. I probed a little further, but he wasn't giving much away. I eventually left the conversation with 'Goodnight, bro. I love you,' and rolled over to sleep.

Trigger Warning – Suicidal incident

It was just after 12 am when I woke with an overwhelming sense of panic, heart pounding, breathing heavily and with thoughts racing around my mind. I'd had plenty of panic attacks in the past, so I knew exactly what to do to calm myself down. I closed my eyes and took control of my inward and outward breaths as my body slowly came to the realisation that I was, in fact, safe. I spoke the name of the Lord into the night, trusting that He is the one who helps me through each moment. I gradually managed to fall back to sleep and hoped to sleep straight through to morning. At around 4 am, I woke up suddenly. I leaned over to check my phone and was surprised to see the numerous missed calls and message notifications. I felt that sinking feeling as I listened to Jacob's suicidal voicemail message. Hearing him cry hit me hard as memories of my mum's frequent suicidal messages came flooding into my mind.

I briefly saw a message from my uncle before taking a deep breath and calling Jacob to see where things were up to. He answered in a hysterical and intoxicated state, telling me how much he missed Mum and how unfair it was that she had died. All I could do was acknowledge how he was feeling and respond with, 'I know, I'm sorry.' I tried my best to keep Jacob calm whilst messaging my uncle and asking him to call the police because my brother was actively planning to commit suicide. Jacob ended the call abruptly, and I sat waiting for him to respond. Ten or twenty minutes passed before he called me back. He was now in the back of a police van and had been arrested! *How on earth did it get to that? I'd asked for the police to be called because I thought they'd get him some mental health help. I thought they were going to take him to a place of safety, not arrest him!*

I frantically called 101 the non-emergency police telephone number) to see what was happening and tried to explain further that my brother had severe mental health problems and needed help. The inspector told me that they'd checked the body cameras of the officers and confirmed that my brother had assaulted one of them. They assured me that he'd be seen by a mental health practitioner and would be looked after. I remained in shock and disbelief for a few hours before managing to get my head around what had happened and having some rest.

The next day was spent making phone calls, trying to get answers. But the police weren't giving me much information. I felt sad that I still hadn't been given an opportunity to speak to my brother to see how he was and to check that he was OK after the suicidal ordeal the night before. I noticed some missed calls from my brother's neighbour, so I called her back as soon as I could. I instantly panicked at the tone of her voice and knew she had some bad news. I had flashbacks of conversations from years earlier, where I'd been told my stepdad and mum were dead. With the pace of the call and the way she was speaking, I genuinely thought she was going to tell me that Jacob was dead. She eventually explained that the police had turned up to collect my brother's spare key because he wouldn't be going back to his flat. She went on to tell me that he had been charged with assault and would be going to prison. I felt a massive sense of relief in knowing that my brother was still alive, but I also felt stunned.

'What do you mean, he's going to prison?' I asked myself the same questions over and over, replaying the scenario in my head and wondering if there was something else I could have done to produce a better outcome. Deep down, I knew I'd done the best I could in that situation, and it wasn't my fault it had panned out the way it had. But I did feel sad about it.

The whole time that Jacob was locked up, I tried to find out where he'd been sent to. But none of the officers would tell me. All I could do at that time was hope and pray that he would be OK. After around five weeks, the prison contacted me because Jacob had tried to kill himself. I was thankful to hear his voice and find out that he was being released in the coming days. I knew it would have been an awful experience for him in prison, and I was glad to know that he'd be able to go home soon.

The first few weeks of the lockdown were a blur as I felt I was in survival mode. I was just about coping with the lack of contact with my brother and the rest of the world. Technology helped a lot, though. It was a great way to stay in touch with friends and others until we were able to meet face-to-face again. I also recognise how blessed I was to not have to do the lock-down alone. I'm so grateful for Jane and Danny, the family I stayed with until the summer of that year. We baked, played games, chatted, worshipped, prayed and exercised together. I especially loved how we would watch inspiring Christian teachings together nearly every night on TV before bed. Not every day of the lockdown felt 'fun', though. It wasn't particularly easy being cooped up in a house, twenty-four hours a day, with the same people for months.

I managed to continue with my studies (which had now been moved online), but I did find sitting and listening to long lectures from behind a screen exceptionally boring. The online dynamic was significantly different to being in a room with other people. I'm thankful that Jane and Danny encouraged me to remain on the course. They helped me stay focused on writing essays, and we had great fun putting together some 'live-action shots' for a class presentation.

CHAPTER 11: INPATIENT INSIGHTS

The pandemic was now in full swing, and the world had no idea when it would end. I attempted to move back to the housing association property but quickly realised I couldn't cope with living there anymore. I chatted with a church friend, and she kindly let me stay with her until I figured out alternative housing arrangements. We prayed together, and within a couple of months, a flat became available in Greater Manchester. I went to view the property and was pleased when the landlords said they were happy for me to move in whenever I'd like.

Just days before Christmas of 2020, I moved into my new place, and as I lay on the mattress on the floor of my bedroom, it didn't seem to matter to me that

I didn't have a bed yet. I now had a safe space to call home, and that is a wonderful, wonderful thing.

I headed over to Rebecca's house on Christmas Eve, ready to spend the next couple of days with her and the family. I woke up that Christmas morning excited about the day ahead. We enjoyed a cooked breakfast and read the nativity story together before heading out to church. Later, we had a luxurious feast! Filled with meat, roast potatoes and other Christmas dinner trimmings, it was magnificent. We exchanged and opened gifts before plonking ourselves in front of the TV to watch a compilation of festive films. It was an all-round lovely day and God used it massively to bring healing around the area of family and Christmas. I was also encouraged when I spent New Year's Eve with friends, and we welcomed in the new year together. There was a great sense of anticipation as we pondered on what the next season would hold.

Much of 2021 was spent rearranging my new flat, continuing with therapy and joining the worship team at Freshfire. Many amazing things happened that year, but there were an overwhelming number of challenges I had to face, too. I know it was a difficult year for many. COVID-19 had impacted everyone's lives in some way or another, and although the lockdown restrictions were now fully lifted, it was clear we all needed a little time to figure out what the new 'norm' looked like.

In September 2021, I had a mental breakdown. I'd struggled for a number of months with suicidal thoughts, and they were feeling too intense to manage at home by myself, so I went into a psychiatric hospital for some help. I expected the time I spent there to be therapeutic, but I quickly realised it was going to be more of a learning opportunity for me.

I was transferred from A&E to the psychiatric ward at around 4 am. The room was bare and cell-like, but the lady who walked me to my room seemed nice enough. There was, however, a collage of photographs on the wall. They were pictures of a young woman and what I assumed were her friends and family. I questioned the nurse about them, wondering if I'd been placed in the wrong room. She told me that the lady was on leave for the weekend and this was only a temporary bed for the night. I chatted briefly with the nurse whilst she did a COVID swab (it was mandatory practice for all new patients at the time), and we got on to the topic of faith. She said she was a Christian, too, so that felt a little reassuring. She left the room, and I tried to get some sleep, but I felt severely anxious in that dark and unknown place. I told the nurse how I was feeling, expecting her to spend some time supporting and reassuring me. I was surprised when she immediately stood up and made her way towards the medicine cabinet, calmly stating that the doctor had prescribed me some medication. I informed her that I knew nothing about a new medication being prescribed and that I didn't feel comfortable taking it because I didn't know what it was. She handed me the tablet, briefly reassuring me it would help with the anxiety I was feeling. I placed it back into her hand and said I would not be taking it. I was a little perplexed as to why she had instantly gone to trying to offer me a pill before listening to or even asking me why I felt anxious. I went back to bed and prayed before slowly drifting off to sleep.

The next morning, I headed towards the nurses' office to ask them some questions about my stay. I was keen to find out when the lady whose bedroom I was sleeping in was expected to return to the ward. I expressed the concerns I had about her returning to find someone else in her bedroom. I felt anxious about how she'd respond and whether she'd kick off verbally or maybe even physically with me. The staff's responses were limited, and it seemed as though they were too busy to explain anything. I asked quite a few times that day, but no further details were given. I went to bed that night feeling ignored and frustrated.

TRIGGER WARNING – SELF-HARM INCIDENT

It was nearing the end of the weekend, and I had a feeling that the lady whose room I was in would show up at the hospital soon. I reminded the staff that I was in her bedroom, and I told them how anxious I felt about it. But again, they brushed off the comments I'd made and didn't take any action. A high-pitched alarm pierced the air as staff ran to another part of the ward. A patient had self-harmed in the bathroom. It must have been a bloody mess, as I saw a staff member strolling across the communal space to throw blood-soaked tissues in a nearby bin. The other residents became visibly distressed at the sight, and I stood there stunned.

Did we all need to see that? Were there no other discreet bins where the dripping tissues could have been placed?

I felt frustrated with how insensitively the situation was being handled, but that soon passed as I saw the lady who'd hurt herself slumped in a chair in the hallway. I felt compassion towards her and asked her if she was OK after what had happened. The staff handed her some wipes and a bandage, and she started to bandage herself up.

I asked the staff why they weren't doing it for her, but she quickly replied with something like, 'Don't worry, I'm used to doing it myself now; they're too busy.' It was honestly so sad to see that this woman had become so used to being treated in that way that, somehow, it was now her 'norm'.

Later that evening, the lady (whose bedroom I was in) returned from her weekend away. I knew she would. I was peacefully eating my dinner when she stormed in and started shouting and swearing at me and demanding for the staff to get me out of her room. I felt on edge and apologised profusely, assuring her it wasn't my fault and that the staff had been the ones who put me in there. The staff attempted to calm the situation down and eventually moved me to another room on the ward. It turned out the new room wasn't actually a bedroom at all, but a therapy room with a makeshift bed in it. I understood now why they'd placed me in that lady's room. There weren't enough beds in the ward for me to be there.

One of the things about the hospital stay I did find enjoyable was chatting with the other patients. I got chatting with a lady who was a similar age to me, and we had a good laugh together. It felt nice to have some fun moments there in amongst the chaos and craziness. That particular lady had been admitted into the psychiatric ward because she was struggling with psychosis. In the early hours of the next morning, she began to show signs of paranoia. I was concerned about what was happening, so I informed the nurses and expected them to spend some time supporting her. I can't say I was surprised when they didn't. I sat with her for a while as she told me some of the thoughts and feelings she was having. She remembered from an earlier conversation that I have a YouTube channel, and she asked me if I would sing some songs. As I started to sing, she visibly became calmer and more relaxed, and soon, we both settled for the night.

The next morning, I went into the communal area to speak with the staff. One of them was sitting on his phone with his feet on the desk, looking unapproachable and disinterested. Others were sitting chatting in the corner. I met with the psychiatrist who was doing the 'morning rounds' and was glad to say that I no longer felt suicidal and was happy to go home. They agreed that was the best thing for me and stated that the psychiatric ward environment isn't always a therapeutic experience for every patient. I scoffed at their statement, but I did acknowledge that the hospital stay had kept me somewhat safe until the suicidal thoughts and feelings had left.

I eagerly packed my things, and my support worker arrived later that day to pick me up.

I was honestly so thankful to be out of there! It took me a few days to recover from the hospital admission, but I was also glad I'd been able to see and feel what a psychiatric ward was like. I know it's an extra experience and insight I have that I can use to bring about awareness and change.

In October 2021, I started going to a mental health café in the local area. The idea of the café was that they'd offer face-to-face support to anyone struggling mentally. I got on particularly well with Lyndsey. She was quirky, funny and down to earth. She had lots of knowledge and experience of the psychiatric world, which made conversations with her easy and enjoyable. It felt helpful to have someone there to listen. And it was an added bonus that she came across as kind and mothering. We'd talk for hours about lots of deep and personal things; not just about things that were going on in my life, but things in her life, too. With the café being a new service, there weren't many rules or boundaries with how often people could attend, so I found myself going there most nights (for weeks at a time).

I noticed I began to get attached to Lyndsey quite quickly and craved spending time with her. There was something about that relationship dynamic that tapped into the trauma wounds I was dealing with at the time. And Lyndsey helped in some ways to soothe me, much like a mother would a child. She would drop me home most nights after the café had closed, and we'd often continue conversations in the car, parked outside my flat for an hour or so until early morning. I found the lack of boundaries with Lyndsey was helpful in some ways because I loved spending time with her, but it soon became apparent that the blurred relational boundaries were actually making the relationships at the café very unsafe for me. I started to act out in unhealthy ways with self-harming and attempting suicide. That cycle went on for many months, into the beginning of 2022.

CHAPTER 12: BREAKING FREE

Ever since I was a girl, I've loved the number 22. I didn't really know why, but I did. Early on in my walk with God, He spoke to me about this number. He spoke to me about healing, deliverance and freedom from the past. He also mentioned newness in relation to the number 22. I thought at the time that He was talking about when I turned 22, but I know now that it was much bigger than that. I believe a huge part of the word He gave me was about the year 2022.

January 2022 was filled with many exciting moments for me. One of the more memorable experiences was when I turned up at a prayer night at a local church. I'd felt quite mentally unwell for a few months prior, so I was pleasantly surprised when the topic of prayer that evening was around mental health. We prayed to see a shift in the minds and hearts of anyone struggling with mental health problems and that they would experience healing and freedom. We also prayed that God would use us where He wants to; to help others. I felt encouraged and strengthened as the meeting ended that night. I planned to drop my friend Talya off at home, and we had an in-depth conversation in the car about the awesomeness of the meeting we'd just attended. As I got closer to Talya's house, I noticed a lady in the middle of the road. She looked visibly distressed, so without hesitation, I pulled over. I asked my friend if she was happy to help me check if the lady needed help. We made our way tentatively towards the lady, asking if she was OK. At that point, she was on the floor crying, and I sat down next to her. I felt led to ask her if she'd like a hug. She nodded before nestling into me and pouring her heart out about the mental breakdown she currently found herself in. Talya and I prayed with her and asked if she needed a lift home. She said she didn't want to be a burden on anyone, but I reminded her that she wasn't being a burden on me, and I was happy to take her home if she'd like that. She agreed to a lift, so Talya and I helped her into the car and dropped her off at home. As I drove back towards Talya's place, we were in absolute awe of what had just happened and how quickly God had answered that evening's prayer of 'use me where you want to use me'.

From February to May of that year, I continued going to the mental health café for support. God used the relationship with Lyndsey to uncover some significant rejection, attachment and abandonment issues. And I knew it was time to deal with them. I had the realisation that I'd placed Lyndsey on a pedestal, as though I were seeing her as the mother figure I desperately needed as a child. But she'd regularly disappoint me by not sticking to things she'd agreed to, and in those moments, I felt reminded of broken promises from my mum. It reminded me of the deep disappointment I felt as a child when my mum didn't hold true to her word. It felt extremely painful to process, and to be quite honest, there were times I wanted to give up. But I knew that I had to keep moving forward. Staying stuck in the trauma wasn't an option anymore!

In May 2022, I watched 'Beauty and the Beast' at the theatre with a friend. I'd arranged to meet with Lyndsey after the show, but she called to let me know that it wasn't going to be possible, and I felt triggered and upset. I cried on the phone with her for nearly an hour as I made my way home and lay in despair on my living room floor. I realise now how dramatic it sounds, but it's worth mentioning that the level of despair I was feeling that night wasn't all about Lyndsey. The situation with Lyndsey had acted as a trigger, bringing difficult memories and emotions to the forefront of my mind. Many of the memories were about my mum. As the phone call with Lyndsey came to an end, I had a strong urge to express what I was feeling through song. With tears streaming down my face, I began to sing and play a melody. What came out sounded like a heart cry from my younger self, the little girl who had suffered so much and had longed to feel loved and wanted. It was a massively healing experience for me. It was cathartic, but it was also very important. I was voicing what my younger self had struggled to articulate back then, but soothing myself in the process. I felt much better afterwards and was wonderfully encouraged by the profound song I had written. I believe the melody and lyrics were very much inspired by God, and although the circumstances that day had been exceptionally difficult, I recognise now how it all helped with the build-up to that restorative moment.

I prayed and asked the Lord if I should record and release the song and I sensed He was saying yes. I tangibly felt the excitement and anticipation within as I attended Freshfire that weekend. At the end of the service, Adam (the leader of Freshfire Church) started sharing prophetic words with people. I waited patiently as he began sharing with me what he felt the Lord was saying. He talked about releasing songs and how God has gifted me to awaken and minister to the little girls and boys in others. I was amazed and started to weep as he spoke those words. The new song I'd written was called 'Little Girl', so it felt like a confirmation from the Lord. Within a few weeks, I had recorded and was ready to release the song.

You can access my songs by scanning this QR code.

SCAN ME

On my mum's death anniversary, I held a song launch party. It was important to me that it was that specific date as a symbol of healing and restoration. I was choosing to claim that the 30th of June was no longer going to be a day of grief but a redeemed and special day. As I looked around the room at those who'd come to support me, I felt overcome with thankfulness. God is so beautiful. I was amazed at the number of women who were there, women whom God has strategically placed in my life to help me sense the love of a mother. There were many layers of healing and restoration symbolised in the room that day. The party being held at Fay and Louise's house was a sure sign of how far we'd all come since the difficult ending at their home just five years earlier. I was blessed and encouraged to be there. As I sang and shared the story of how I'd written 'Little Girl', I knew God had done something ginormous in my heart. A deep and precious healing.

A few days after the excitement of the song launch party, I felt very low in mood. *'I'll go to the café to see Lyndsey'*, I thought to myself, though I knew the Lord was prompting me not to see her anymore. The attachment I had with her was no longer healthy or necessary. Initially, I thought it was unfair, and I didn't feel ready to stop going to the café yet, so I continued going for a few more weeks. A self-harm incident occurred at the café, and the decision was made that I could no longer access that specific service. In some way, it was helpful that the decision had been made for me, but the separation from Lyndsey felt excruciatingly painful to begin with. However, after some time and some intentional processing, I managed to let go of the attachment I had to Lyndsey and was thankful to receive healing and move on from that place. Amazingly, God used all that I went through at the café for good. It didn't necessarily feel good in the middle of it, but it's incredible how God healed so many memories and wounds that had been triggered and brought to the surface in that season. One of the major things I learned through that twelve-month process is that there is purpose in the pain and purpose in the process. It doesn't always feel easy, but it is always worth it.

In the summer of 2022, Freshfire led an Alpha Course, a course that explores the basics of the Christian faith through teaching and discussions. I was super excited when my brother Jacob said he'd like to come along, and he seemed to be taking in and understanding more about God. In one of the sessions, we touched on the topic of forgiveness. I was reminded of many who had hurt and abused me in the past, as well as times I'd hurt others, too. I'm so thankful to have received complete forgiveness from God. Remembering that I'm forgiven often helps me to forgive others quicker. In that Alpha session,

I thought specifically about Peggy and Basil (the foster carers who abused me in my childhood). I was reminded how, over the years, I'd said out loud, 'I forgive you both, and I bless you. I pray that you repent and turn to God.' You see, although I don't agree with the way they treated me and the other children, I don't hate them. I understand that Peggy and Basil were clearly very broken people, and I genuinely feel compassion towards them. During the session on forgiveness, I questioned and considered if I'd forgiven them both fully.

The next morning, I woke up and got ready to meet a friend. For some reason, she was running late, so I asked God what He wanted me to do instead. I felt He asked me to drive to Basil and Peggy's house, to knock on their door and tell them that I forgive them. So, I grabbed my car keys and set off. It was approximately a forty-minute car journey, and I felt peaceful as I drove, singing and praying aloud. I pulled up to the street, spotting the pylon that Liam and I used to play on as youngsters. It suddenly hit me how big a thing this was!

I parked outside the house, staring at the windows as thoughts raced through my mind. I rushed out of the car, knowing that if I thought about it for too much longer, then I might have chickened out. I made my way towards the front door and knocked. A few seconds passed before a man appeared in the doorway. 'Do

Peggy and Basil live here?' I asked sheepishly. From his response, I could tell he had no clue who or what I was talking about. So, I quickly said 'No problem', thanked him and headed back towards my car. I hesitated as I put the key in the lock and thought to myself, '*I'm here now; I may as well have a little wander around.*'

As I walked the streets I used to play on as a girl, I felt such peace and calm. I knew in that moment that I'd fully forgiven those foster carers. I sensed God telling me that they no longer have a hold on me and that by His Grace, I'm free. I continued walking down the steep hill that I used to sledge on with friends, as God revealed more and more fun memories to me. He reminded me of the joy and the laughter. He spoke over me again His promise of 'restoring the years that the locusts had eaten'. I cried and thanked Him, filled with gratitude and wonder. I let out a sigh of relief as I thanked Him for the fact that I'm no longer where I used to be. I pondered in my heart the reality that every day with Jesus truly is an adventure.

CHAPTER 13: MONUMENTAL MOMENTS

Another monumental moment for me in 2022 was celebrating my graduation. I received a Certificate of Higher Education and had the honour of wearing a cap and gown and taking part in the whole graduation ceremony experience. I was happy I graduated on the same day as Melisa, too. It was very special to be sharing such a significant moment with her. It was a massive achievement, but most importantly, it was another restorative experience. I felt like I'd failed in some ways during school in the care system, and I'd somehow believed a lie that I was stupid. That graduation day, I came to the realisation that I'm definitely not stupid and that God has, in fact, gifted me with intelligence and wisdom.

In August of that year, I felt inspired to create a new song. As I sang and played, I envisaged Jesus as the bridegroom and me as the bride. The lyrics flowed from a place of intimacy and adoration as I focused on the truth that God is always holding me close. After I'd jotted down the lyrics and recorded the melody, I couldn't help but wonder if this was another song I would release someday (you'll read more about this soon).

ENCOUNTER WEEKEND

For the few weeks that followed, I struggled massively with low mood. Although I didn't know exactly how or when it would shift, I was expectant that it would. I knew there was an upcoming 'encounter' weekend with the church, and I anticipated that it would help bring the change I was hoping for.

The idea of encounter weekends with Freshfire is to intentionally set aside time to seek and encounter God. It's an opportunity to allow the Holy Spirit to reveal and heal any wounds as well as help you get rid of any spiritual baggage that may have been holding you back.

On the 8th of September 2022, I made my way to the building where the encounter weekend was happening. I felt like I arrived that first night in a very dark and low place, desperately knowing I needed God to do something miraculous. The team welcomed us and outlined what we could expect over the coming days. I felt very dissociated but became more engaged as we went into a time of prayer and worship. I felt an immediate shift, as though I were breathing out all negativity. Adam said he was sensing pockets of joy in a certain spot in the room, so in faith, I walked over to that area to pray and receive. I felt the presence of God so strongly that I fell backwards. It was as though liquid joy was being poured into the depths of my soul. I couldn't help but smile and laugh. The scripture, 'the joy of the Lord is my strength', was mentioned, and that resonated deeply with me. As I lay on the floor, I sensed so much peace, joy and love. It was truly amazing.

As the evening went on, the praying and shouting got louder and more intense. I felt scared and triggered as flashbacks from the past overwhelmed my senses. Interestingly, the things that people were praying loudly about had to do with spirits that try to invoke fear in people.

TRIGGER WARNING – SELF-HARM AND SUICIDAL IDEATION

I went outside to try to calm down, but I suddenly had strong thoughts and urges to jump over the stairwell. I recognise now that it was very much a spiritual attack. I ran back inside, locked myself in the bathroom cubicle and sat on the floor crying. I remembered there was something sharp in my bag, so I took it out and started to cut my arm with it. My friend Hope Smith (who is a leader at Freshfire) knocked on the door to check if I was OK, but I was reluctant to let her in. I felt embarrassed by what I'd done. Eventually, I opened the door to accept help from her and the other church team members. Hope and Grace dropped me off at home and prayed for me in the car before I headed inside to sleep.

The next morning, I woke up at around 4 am to hear God saying, 'You don't need to push the boundaries anymore. I'm never going to leave you.' I wept as I allowed what I'd heard to sink deeper into my being. I knew that what He'd just spoken was exactly what I needed to hear that day.

I drove to the church for day two of 'encounter', expectant for more breakthroughs and freedom. I was slightly apprehensive because of what had happened the night before, but that soon dissipated as I encountered Father God in the session on identity. God showed me a picture of a mirror, a bronze old-fashioned style one with fancy-looking edges. As I took a closer look to see what was in the reflection, I saw myself as a warrior! A daughter of the King, surrounded by Holy Spirit fire. I took out my scrapbook and began drawing what I'd seen. I drew myself, wearing a long purple robe with black boots. In one hand, I was wielding a sword, and in the other hand, something that resembled the Olympic torch with a flame. Not forgetting the Holy Spirit fire surrounding me! I was amazed and extremely thankful for such a mighty revelation and encounter.

As the weekend continued, we had a variety of sessions on things like forgiveness, sex, soul ties and the Father's heart. One of the sessions I particularly liked was where we broke off generational curses and chose to receive our generational blessings. It was powerful and monumental. I also noticed at some point during the programme, the fear I had of germs had fallen away. I was no longer feeling the compulsion to use hand sanitiser every time I touched something. I thanked Jesus for setting me free! The final part of the programme involved us sharing a meal to celebrate all that God had done. It was beautiful.

For several weeks after the encounter weekend, I felt like I was walking around in a bubble of euphoria. It was amazing. I knew that at some point, I would feel other emotions again, and I reminded myself that it doesn't change what God has done and the freedom I've received.

In October 2022, I began an 'interesting' journey with group therapy. Throughout the majority of the first session, I felt overwhelmed and distressed. At the end of the four hours, I sat in my car and cried. I chatted with God about it. I was open and honest with Him, saying, 'I really don't think this group therapy is for me, Lord. It felt too much. If I'm not gonna get anything out of it, then I don't want to keep attending those sessions.' I caught a glance of myself in the rearview mirror, realising how much I looked and sounded like a toddler having a tantrum. I sensed God gently nudging me, reminding me that it's not all about me and what I can 'get' out of things. He showed me some reasons as to why He wanted me to keep attending the therapy. At that moment (even though it felt tough), I chose to submit to Him and said yes to continuing with the group therapy journey.

Christmas With Mary

I made plans with my friend Mary for Christmas that year. Mary and I had gotten to know each other more in the previous months, serving on the worship team at

Freshfire and enjoying songwriting together at my house. We planned to make this Christmas super festive and fun. She drove over to my place on Christmas Eve, and we spent the evening making gingerbread men, eating takeout, drinking cocoa and watching random festive films. It was great! On Christmas morning, we visited a local church for a special time of worship and fellowship. I briefly saw Rebecca (the friend I'd spent Christmas with for the past few years), telling her I'd drop by her house at around 6 pm. Mary and I rushed off after the service to sing and serve at a Christmas dinner for care leavers. One of the things I love to do with Mary is sing. She has such an anointed voice, so I was extremely excited at the thought of us ministering at the care leavers event together. On arrival, we were informed that the guests had been doing karaoke for the best part of an hour. As we set up to sing, I think people assumed we were just continuing with the karaoke. It felt quite awkward to begin with, but I was encouraged when I saw a young lady at the front who seemed mesmerised and peaceful throughout the Christmas-themed setlist.

Next on the agenda was Christmas dinner. Mary and I asked if they needed help to serve the food, but they had it all sorted, so we sat down at a table and started chatting with guests and volunteers. Within minutes, we'd been served a full Christmas dinner with lashings of gravy. It was scrumptious! We enjoyed our desserts before helping facilitate the foodbank station that had been set up for the guests. I started to feel a little tired, so I was pleased when we were told that the event was nearly over and we could leave whenever we'd like. We waved goodbye, packed away the keyboard, and Mary dropped me back at home. She headed off to spend the rest of the evening at her mum's, and I walked over to spend the evening with Rebecca and her family.

We exchanged and opened presents before sitting in front of the TV to watch something christmassy. As I perched on the sofa and looked around the room, I knew that something felt different. I couldn't pinpoint exactly what it was, but I knew I felt uncomfortable. My friendship with Rebecca had felt strained for the previous twelve months, so I guessed it had something to do with that. She'd become increasingly busy with work, and we'd spent significantly less time chatting and meeting up with one another. At the beginning of our friendship, we were very close. We'd spent lots of time together and responded relatively quickly to each other's messages and calls. But that had changed now, and I struggled to come to terms with that for around eighteen months. Anyway, I managed to stay at Rebecca's house for the rest of that Christmas evening. I headed home at around 11.30 pm, and as I lay in bed that night, I felt thankful to have made it through such an emotional rollercoaster of a day.

CHAPTER 14: SILENCED NO MORE

I welcomed in the new year with friends. We got creative, writing words of expectation and hope for the things we'd like to do and see in 2023. One of the things on my list was the deep desire to release more songs.

The first week into 2023, I felt a little frustrated. I had a song ready to record and release, but for some reason, it just wasn't coming together as quickly as I'd hoped it would. I decided to hand the whole process over to God, saying, 'If You want me to release this new song, then please open the right doors with the right people.' Within a week or so, a friend contacted me. He mentioned how the Lord had spoken to him about offering me some free studio time to record and produce a track. And yet again, I was in awe of the faithfulness of Jesus!

The studio experience was full of fun and special moments. I arrived slightly earlier than everyone else, so I headed up to the room to get settled. The team showed up a little while later, and we began the session. I felt such joy and peace as we worked on the track together, laughing and sharing stories with one another. Five hours flew by, and before we left, I had the chance to listen to some of what we'd created. I expected to receive the finalised version in around two months because the producer was busy working on some other projects, but I was pleasantly surprised when I received the song in less than four weeks. I felt incredibly thankful to have been given such a great opportunity and was amazed at how quickly it had all come together. It was a good reminder that God's ways really are higher and better, and His timing is perfect.

Another thing I've learned about God's ways is that they're not always 'conventional'. A great example of this would be the group therapy that He encouraged me to keep attending. I struggled so much emotionally in those sessions that for three or four days afterwards, I felt like I needed to recover. In your natural mind, you may think, 'Why would God want you to keep going somewhere that is having that effect on you?' Trust me, I asked myself (and God) that question many times! But each time I asked Him if I should continue with the group therapy, I felt His answer was yes. He reminded me that I was in a process and that it was important for me not to run away from it, even if, at times, it felt difficult.

In February 2023, there was a particularly awful group therapy session. Someone was making passive-aggressive statements about me, and I felt unsafe. It triggered some difficult memories of when I was bullied or spoken down to as a child. In similar situations in the past, there were times I'd stay silent as a form of self-protection. I had to make a choice that day. Was I going to remain in a triggered and traumatised state? Or was I going to overcome it and speak up? I chose to speak up. I was encouraged and pleased with how I'd articulated effectively and respectfully what was going on for me. I went home that evening, feeling thankful to Jesus for growth and healing.

From that moment on, I've continued to grow in using my voice and being more articulate, even in the midst of heightened emotions. Would I have personally chosen for that freedom to happen in such a painful way? Probably not. However, I believe that God knows best, and I thank Him for the healing, anyway. His ways aren't always conventional, but He is always good.

Another monumental healing experience for me was when I met up with Rose. Rose had been one of my social workers as a child. I bumped into her in a park in 2022 and exchanged contact details with her, with the intention of meeting up sometime in the future. The time had now come around for it to happen!

On the 4th of April 2023, I woke up feeling really nervous about the meet-up. I knew I was ready to have the difficult conversations with Rose, but I still felt a little apprehension. We met at a local park, and the conversation flowed relatively naturally. We started chatting about how I'd gotten on since leaving the care system, before moving on to discussing some of the good and challenging things from my childhood. I told her some of the horrific ways I'd been treated in the children's home, and although she seemed saddened, she wasn't hugely surprised. She apologised for what had happened, and I acknowledged that it wasn't her fault, but I appreciated the apology, anyway. Rose reassured me that she wasn't aware of the abuse I had gone through and that if she had been, she would have done something about it. I had conflicting emotions in that moment because I knew I'd definitely spoken up at times about what was happening to me back then. But for some reason, it hadn't been properly heard. *What was the reason for that? Was it because I was a child? Were the adults' versions of events automatically believed over the child's version?*

I then had another realisation. I don't think I shared the whole story of each incident with Rose when she visited me in the children's home. I'd had discussions with other adults before her about the way I was being treated, and I'd often not been believed. It suddenly made sense why my younger self struggled to tell Rose the details of the horrors I was facing in those childhood years. I was scared to not be believed again. And I was scared that the abuse would continue. But not anymore!

I'm thankful I was given the opportunity to voice to Rose (as an adult) what I'd struggled to voice to her as a child. Those conversations with her helped me to process and move forward from the re-traumatised place I was in. I actively chose to forgive and let go of those who had mistreated me in my childhood. I recognised that meeting up with Rose was another restorative and healing encounter for me.

Rose and I continued to chat, recounting funny stories of the antics I used to get up to. She reminded me of how I'd missed practically all of year nine at school and how they wanted me to sit a literacy test. They were incredibly shocked when the results came back, and my reading age was 18 years plus (I was only 13 at the time). Rose said it was amazing how I'd missed so much schooling but was still incredibly bright. I loved seeing her face light up when I told her I had, in fact, sat and passed all of my GCSEs.

One of the precious things I learned through meeting up with Rose that day was that even though I 'felt' very alone as a child, I wasn't. There were many who journeyed alongside me in my childhood, fighting on my behalf. Back then, I felt so alone and struggled to see the light amongst the intensity of the darkness that surrounded me. But I see it now. I once was blind, but now I see. Such amazing grace!

Rose was by far the best social worker I had throughout my care system experience. Not only did she fight for me, but she worked incredibly hard. She put in extra hours, energy and effort, and I'm extremely thankful for that.

I also want to say a big thank you to the many social workers now who work incredibly hard and go the extra mile. Thank you to those who spend countless hours with children who've been through pain and trauma, being a source of safety and stability for them. Thank you.

Thankyou

CHAPTER 15: DEEP-LEVEL HEALING

Many people have said to me, 'Writing about what you've been through must be so cathartic.' I often chuckle in response to that statement. Although I agree on some level that writing about things from the past has been somewhat cathartic, there's much more to it than that. Writing this book has not been plain sailing. Many of the stories I've shared within these pages were, at some point, too painful to even think about. I often felt as though I were reliving the experiences as I wrote about them in this book. However, one of the beautiful things about having God in my life is that, when that happened, He didn't leave me to struggle with the difficult feelings alone. He led me through many deep-level healing encounters, bringing healing to different memories and setting me free from the pain and trauma of them. I'll share an example with you.

TRIGGER WARNING – SEXUAL ASSAULT

On the 19th of May 2023, I was remembering and writing about an experience I had aged 16 when I got drunk with a girl from the children's home, and a guy took advantage of me in the local park. You will have read this story earlier in the book. As I was writing about it, I felt overcome with guilt and shame. I felt as though it was all my fault because I was drunk, and I hadn't said no or struggled with the man when he was doing what he was doing. I felt myself going into a flash-back experience. I was sitting on my sofa in May 2023, but part of me felt as though I was back in 2010 with that man in the park. It was as though I was feeling and experiencing that trauma again. I felt myself becoming more and more overwhelmed. I desperately repeated the name of Jesus and, at that moment, felt led to call a friend from Freshfire Church. I told her exactly what was going on for me. I told her how I was feeling and the thoughts I was having about it all being my fault because I'd put myself in that situation by getting drunk. My friend calmly reassured me there and then that I was safe. She reminded me that I was a 16-year-old girl at the time, and the man had supplied me with alcohol, likely with the intention of using me in the way that he did. She also reassured me that I was not in a place to be able to consent to sexual activity because I was intoxicated. He took advantage of me, and I was not to blame.

She asked me if I would like to invite Jesus into that memory, and I agreed. As I prayed and focused on Jesus throughout the flashback, I saw Him by my side as I was lying on the cold, damp grass. I felt calm and peaceful, knowing that He was beside me, holding my hand. In that memory, I gave all the shame and disgust to Jesus. I gave him the feelings of unforgiveness, anger and injustice. I surrendered the blame that I'd been holding onto towards the girl who'd left me, the man who'd assaulted me and the policemen who hadn't taken my disclosure seriously enough. And I said aloud, 'I choose to forgive them all.'

I asked Jesus, 'What are you gonna do with those things I've just given you?' and I saw a picture of Him rolling it all up into a ball. He threw it far away, to a place where it wasn't visible anymore. 'It's gone now,' He said reassuringly. I knew He wasn't dismissing what I'd gone through. It's as though He was showing me a visual representation of the fact that I'm now free from that traumatic experience. It no longer has a hold on me.

I also gave Jesus the lies I'd been believing about myself because of what had happened to me. I asked

Him what truth He would like to exchange those lies with, and I heard Him say, 'I've given you the bravery and the courage to stand.' I was sprawled on the floor in my flat at that point, so when I heard Him say that, I stood up. I sensed Him saying that sharing these stories in my book will help set others free. Particularly those who feel or have felt it was their fault when they were abused.

I'm thankful to say that if ever I think back about the story recounted above, I no longer feel emotional pain about it. I've been healed from that trauma.

The technique/tool that my friend used to help me process the trauma memory above is something she learned through the Restoration Centre. The Restoration Centre is a ministry that specialises in deep-level healing, amongst other things. You can find their contact details on the list of organisations at the end of this book.

CHAPTER 16:
OUT WITH THE OLD, IN WITH THE NEW

In May 2023, I had a difficult experience at Freshfire. I'd pushed myself to go to church that morning, mostly because there was a meeting planned for afterwards that I really didn't want to miss. I sat in the room during the worship and the preaching, feeling disengaged and depressed. A few people tried to comfort and reassure me, but I felt as though I was in my own little world. I rushed out at the end of the service and headed to the local coffee shop, where I'd planned to meet with Adam and Hope.

The shop was busy and loud, and I could feel the sensory overload intensifying. As Adam and Hope arrived, they grabbed a drink, and we sat at the table to chat. I sat there in silence, feeling dissociated and overwhelmed. Hope tried to engage in conversation with me, but I struggled to respond to her. I was able to articulate in my head exactly what I wanted to say aloud, but the words just refused to come out of my mouth. Internally, I started beating myself up for not being able to verbalise there and then what was going on for me. It was an incredibly difficult interaction for all of us. After many attempts from Hope to encourage me to talk, they both thought it was best to draw the meeting to a close. As Adam and Hope left the shop, I sat there sobbing for a few moments. I felt depths of despair as thoughts and images from my past flashed through my mind. What had just happened reminded me of some rejection and abandonment from the past, and although in those moments it felt painful and hard, the situation had brought to light some things that I was then able to process and heal from with Jesus.

As part of that processing, I wrote another song called 'I love you, Mum'. The song helped me express some of the difficult things I'd wanted to say to my mum as a child. Questions I wanted to ask her but never quite felt able to. It was an extremely tough thing to do, but it was also therapeutic. The Lord used it to bring deeper healing to my soul, and within a few days, I started to feel much better.

Shortly after, I had a chat with Hope about the meeting. I found the conversation both productive and restorative as we discussed our perspectives and views on what had happened. I was hugely encouraged when she asked me if I'd like to put a document together with ideas of how to make Sunday services an even safer space for those working through mental health difficulties. It was amazing to see how such a difficult interaction had been able to be used for the good of myself and others.

Throughout June of that year, I noticed countless situations that triggered feelings of deep disappointment within me. I sensed it was God intentionally uncovering some wounds around disappointment and loss. I believe He was allowing me to feel and process those things, not to hurt me but to bring healing.

On the 3rd of July 2023, disappointment hit me hard. I'd really been looking forward to a prayer ministry appointment with a couple of ladies from church, but for some reason, they had to cancel. Interestingly, the session was going to be around the feelings of disappointment related to my childhood. I quickly realised that this healing encounter was going to happen differently from how I expected.

On Friday 7th of July, I went to a 'Revival Night' conference that was being hosted by a prayer-based ministry in Manchester. I had a beautiful encounter with the Lord, where I saw Him standing next to me with His hand out. I joined my hand to His and tangibly felt His hand in mine throughout the worship time. I felt refreshed and invigorated, and that night, as I slept, I had a dream about the man who had been preaching. In the dream, he looked and pointed at me, saying, 'You're free now from the bondage of the past!'

The following morning, I ministered my 'Little Girl' song at a women's brunch and led a time of worship. It was an inspiring and encouraging experience for me and the other ladies who attended. I was very thankful for the opportunity and was extremely excited to see what that evening's 'Revival Night' was going to entail.

I arrived for the evening session to find there were no chairs set out in the middle of the room. I guessed it was to make space for more people to attend the session, but I tingled with anticipation as I recounted the dream earlier that day, where there were no chairs visible. I was even more amazed when the message the preacher shared that evening was about getting free from emotional/psychological prisons. He was so specific that, at times, I felt he was talking directly to me.

He declared, 'You are not a victim anymore.' He led us in a time of prayer, and I was reminded of my freedom and the importance of declaring and truly believing that I am indeed free.

CELEBRATING MY 30TH!

A few days later, it was my joy-filled 30th birthday. It was a monumental day for me, and I'm thankful I celebrated it the way that I did. Months earlier, I'd prayed about where I should have it and what it should look like. I felt led to have a picnic-style event at Heaton Park in Manchester with some of my friends and family. As the day drew closer, the weather became more unpredictable, with a storm forecast slap bang in the middle of the day. I considered changing the venue but knew that I was supposed to celebrate my 30th in the park, no matter the weather. So, I chose to make the most of the situation and bought a selection of brightly coloured waterproof ponchos (just in case it rained). I noticed a significant difference in the way I was handling the unpredictability of the day and felt encouraged. Years ago, I likely would have had an emotional meltdown and cancelled the plans. But instead, I danced and sang in the rain with my friends. Thankfully, there were plenty of sunny moments, too. I felt as though the Lord was speaking to me through the weather that day, reminding me that no matter what the weather is like, I can remain joyful.

Amongst the people who came was my childhood social worker, Rose. It meant a lot to me that she had made the effort to see me on my 30th birthday. It was a stark reminder of just how far I have come and how much my life has changed since leaving the care system (for the better, of course). There were moments throughout the day when I looked around in awe and contentment, realising just how blessed I am. As I stood there with my friends, sheltered beneath an oak tree, I was overwhelmed with thankfulness. It was a truly beautiful day. I am blessed and grateful to have celebrated thirty years of life, and I believe I will celebrate many more years.

AS ONE CHAPTER ENDS, ANOTHER BEGINS

I grappled for a few months with how, where and when to end this book. I finally settled on the idea of ending it with the story of my 30th birthday. Trying to condense thirty years of experiences into only a few chapters has been an intense yet liberating adventure. I'm sure you've been on somewhat of an adventure yourself while reading through these pages!

When I look back at how far I've come, I can't help but be amazed. I'm so thankful for the healing, restoration and newness of life I've been given. I'm grateful that although my life isn't perfect, it does continue to get better and better. I know there are still things I have to work on and process. But in comparison to where I started, I'm sure you can agree that I've come a very long way.

I hope that the stories in this book have encouraged you to know that whatever you're going through or have gone through, there is always hope! Even if, at times, you may struggle to see or feel it. I want to encourage you to hope again. I encourage you to open your eyes to the possibility that even if your story has felt dark and difficult so far, it doesn't have to continue or end that way. Change is possible!

If you've felt stirred by the stories I've shared about Jesus and want to get to know Him for yourself, that's possible, too. You can simply chat with Him, as you would a friend, and tell Him you'd like to get to know Him. I've also added the 'Alpha Course' details at the end of this book, under the **List of Organisations/ Websites/Resources** (if you are interested in learning more about the Christian faith).

Keep Updated

So, you may be wondering, 'What are you going to do next?' I have lots of ideas and plans! And although I can't tell you everything that my future holds, there are some things I know for sure.

Of course, I'll continue to write and release songs. I'll keep singing, creating, growing and loving. And I also believe that this will be the first book of many! If you'd like to keep updated on my journey, for example, regarding upcoming books and songs, you can check out my social media pages at www.linktr.ee/esther.grace.xo

Or you can scan this QR code.

SCAN ME

I'm also very excited to tell you that my business 'Mighty Oaks' is now up and running. I provide workshops, talks and other services to those working with looked-after children, as well as those who support adults with mental health challenges (though it won't be limited to that). One of the aims of my business is that people will gain a deeper understanding of mental health and trauma. Trauma-informed care reduces the likelihood of further traumatisation of those who are currently reliant on others for support.

If you'd like to find out more about the services
I provide, please go to
www.mightyoaks.net

Or you can scan this QR code
to visit my website directly!

SCAN ME

List of Organisations/ Websites/Resources

Alpha Course: For those wanting to explore the basics of Christianity

www.alpha.org.uk

ChildLine: Support for anyone under 19 in the UK (you can talk about anything, big or small)

08001111

Mercy UK: Christian Mental Health and Wellbeing Charity (online resources and support)

www.mercyuk.org
01535642042

Mind: Mental Health Charity (free online resources for mental health)

www.mind.org.uk

National Domestic Abuse Helpline (for men)

08088010327

www.mensadviceline.org.uk

National Domestic Abuse Helpline (for women)

08082000247

www.nationaldahelpline.org.uk

Restoration Centre: Healing and Deliverance Ministry (mentioned in Chapter 15)

www.linktr.ee/RestorationCentre

Samaritans: A confidential phone service available to anyone experiencing loneliness, mental health issues, or other personal difficulties.

116123

SHOUT: A confidential 24/7 text service for those struggling with mental health

text SHOUT to 85258

The Maggie Oliver Foundation: Support for adults who have experienced sexual abuse

www.themaggieoliverfoundation.com

RECOMMENDED BOOKS:

Author – Carolyn Bramhall:

'An Introduction to Dissociative Identity Disorder'
'Am I a Good Girl Yet?'
'Connecting the Fragments'
'Your Personal Growth Course'
'Intelligent Loving' (Carolyn's most recent book to date)

Please contact Carolyn if you'd like to purchase any of her books:

www.carolynbramhall01@gmail.com

About the Author

Esther Grace was born in Manchester, UK in 1993. She spent most of her childhood in the care system and now enjoys sharing stories and insights from her lived experiences to inform, inspire and impact others. Esther is extremely passionate about her faith in Jesus. Having experienced the life-transforming power of His love, she is passionate about seeing others healed and set free, too. Esther is a singer and worship leader and enjoys spending valuable time with friends and loved ones. Esther founded Mighty Oaks in 2024, offering workshops and services to those supporting adults with mental health challenges, as well as those working with looked-after children.